THE GUINNESS
ENCYCLOPAEDIA
OF
GAMES, PUZZLES
& PASTIMES

THE GUINNESS ENCYCLOPAEDIA OF GAMES, PUZZLES & PASTIMES

GUINNESS PUBLISHING

Editor: Honor Head
Design: Clive Sutherland

© Victorama Ltd. and Guinness Publishing Ltd. 1988
Reprinted 1990

Published in Great Britain by Guinness Publishing Ltd.,
33 London Road, Enfield, Middlesex.

Printed and bound in Great Britain by
Mackays of Chatham

'Guinness' is a registered trade mark of
Guinness Publishing Ltd.

British Library Cataloguing in Publication Data

Guinness encyclopaedia of games,
   puzzles & pastimes
   1. Games — Dictionaries
   1. Title
   790   GV174

   ISBN 0-85112-432-1

Picture Acknowledgements
Page 85 Tim Brooke-Taylor, Epic Records
MPL Communications Ltd, Pictorial Press Ltd.
Page 107 RCA Ltd.
Page 111 SIRE
Page 192 National Film Archive Stills Library,
Twentieth-Century Fox
Page 193 London Weekend Television, TV-am.

Contents

Introduction

The Guinness Encyclopaedia of Games, Puzzles & Pastimes is packed with games, puzzles and activities of all kinds, to suit every member of the family from eight — and the under-eights — to eighty. Each alphabetical section contains a wide variety of fascinating material, with puzzles and quizzes of varying difficulty, and games and activities ranging from amusing party games and magic tricks to quiet pastimes for one player only.

Puzzles in the book include word puzzles, mathematical puzzles, picture puzzles, logic puzzles, whodunnit puzzles, coin puzzles, matchstick puzzles, riddles and quizzes. Word puzzles include crosswords, word-searches, acrostics, spelling and the meanings of words; mathematical puzzles range from simple number puzzles to substitution puzzles, number squares, brainteasers and logic puzzles. Picture puzzles include a wide range, from simple spot-the-difference illustrations to optical illusions and observation tests; and there are quizzes on sport, music, cinema, animals and television, as well as a host of general knowledge trivia challenges.

Games in the book include old favourites as well as many new ones destined to become favourites. There are parlour games, children's party games, racing games, ball games, calculator games, word games spoken and written, pencil and paper games, team games, indoor and outdoor games, games for beaches and holidays, card games, dice games, domino games, games for children who are unwell, quiet games, noisy games, silly games, and games which require a good deal of thought.

There is a host of exciting activities, too, including solving codes and ciphers, playing magic tricks and April Fool jokes, learning how to juggle and do impersonations, and making music.

There is something to suit every mood and occasion, and the book is the ideal companion on a family holiday, at a Christmas gathering, in school holiday times, wet weekends or any other time when children — and their elders — are at a loss as to how to occupy themselves. It will provide many happy and entertaining hours, and is a book no family can possibly afford to be without.

Amazing!

Here's a corny maze to start with. Go in at the top by the entry arrow, and work your way down to the exit arrow at the bottom.

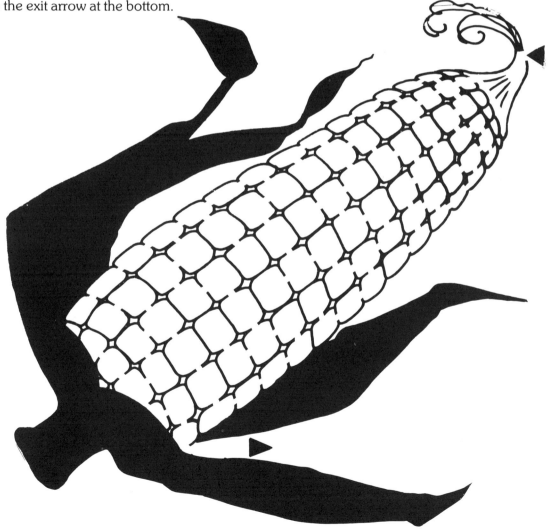

America Ahoy!

The United States

All the states listed below can be traced out in this word-search puzzle. The words can be read across, down or diagonally, either forwards or backwards, but they are always in straight lines. You may find it easier to trace them if you use a pencil and a ruler.

ALASKA
ARIZONA
DELAWARE
GEORGIA
HAWAII
IDAHO
ILLINOIS
IOWA
KANSAS
LOUISIANA
MAINE
MARYLAND

MINNESOTA
MISSISSIPPI
NEBRASKA
NEW YORK
NORTH CAROLINA
NORTH DAKOTA
OHIO
PENNSYLVANIA
TEXAS
UTAH
WASHINGTON
WYOMING

```
W A S H I N G T O N U T A H
Y I A N A I S I U O L K R N
O N S Y D N A L Y R A M I O
M A I C J W P E N N A A Z R
I V O D O Y L L S T K I O T
N L N I I N V A O W L N N H
G Y I S H P S K T M X E A C
K S L A O B A I G R O E G A
R N L X J D L K N Z P W O R
O N I E H B D I I A W A H O
Y E X T M I N N E S O T A L
W P R K P E R A W A L E D I
E O M I S S I S S I P P I N
N E B R A S K A A L A S K A
```

American English

The Americans and the British speak the same language. Or do they? Here is a list of ordinary British English words. What are their American equivalents?

1. Bath.
2. Biscuit.
3. Candy floss.
4. Car bonnet.
5. Chips.
6. Cot.
7. Crisps.
8. Dual carriageway.
9. Funfair.
10. Hair grip.
11. Holiday.
12. Ice lolly.
13. Lorry.
14. Nought.
15. Roundabout (road).
16. Skipping rope.
17. Tap.
18. Underground.
19. Vest.
20. Wardrobe.

American American

1. Which river flows through the Grand Canyon?
2. In which city is Hollywood?
3. What are the five Great Lakes of North America?
4. What is the national bird of America?
5. The Rocky Mountains run down the western side of North America. Which range of mountains runs down the eastern side?
6. How many dimes are there in a dollar?
7. With which sport is the American League concerned?
8. Where is the Statue of Liberty?
9. Where was the Battle of the Alamo fought?
10. When is Thanksgiving Day?

Person to Person

Can you work out the names of these famous Americans of past and present?

1. HAG GREW, NOTING S.O.E.
2. JAN ON FADE.
3. LOW KICK, HILL BID.
4. RON MAY, NO MILER.
5. I CHARM BALL ANON.
6. O, DO WALL, YEN.
7. HEY FOR N.D.R.
8. CRY AN AGE, ANN.

City States

In which American states are the following cities?

1. Birmingham.
2. Boston.
3. Cheyenne.
4. Chicago.
5. Las Vegas.
6. Memphis.
7. Pittsburgh.
8. Salt Lake City.
9. Seattle.
10. Tampa.

Flying the Flag

Which of these flags is the true American flag?

Yankee Doodles

These drawings all represent things connected with America — they may be places, objects or simply American expressions. How many can you recognize?

April Fool

Loose Ends

If you want to prepare a trick for 1 April, or if you just want to have fun with your family or friends, then try this one. All you need is a jacket with an inside pocket, a reel of thread and a needle.

Thread the needle and push it through from the inside to the outside of the jacket. Don't cut off the end of the thread, but put the reel in the inside pocket. Remove the needle and put it away carefully so no one will stick it into themselves. Now all you need is a victim on whom to play the trick.

The ideal person is someone who fusses around you, and is likely to notice a loose thread coming out of your jacket — possibly your mother. She will see the thread, and say, 'Come here, let me pull this thread out of your coat, it looks so untidy.' You should pretend to protest, to make it seem as if you are not playing a trick. Then, when your mother starts to pull the thread, she will be amazed, for it will go on and on, as the reel unwinds in your pocket! That's the time to say, 'April Fool!' — if it is April Fool's Day, of course!

Big Spider

Here's a trick you can play in the classroom or at home. Pretend to stare fixedly at a corner of the room, with a look of horror on your face, and when anyone looks to see what is the matter with you, say, 'Aaaarrrggghhh! Look at that *huge* spider in the corner! Help!'

When everyone starts to get very squeamish and shows signs of wanting to climb on the furniture, or if a brave soul ventures to take a closer look, call out brightly, 'April Fool!'

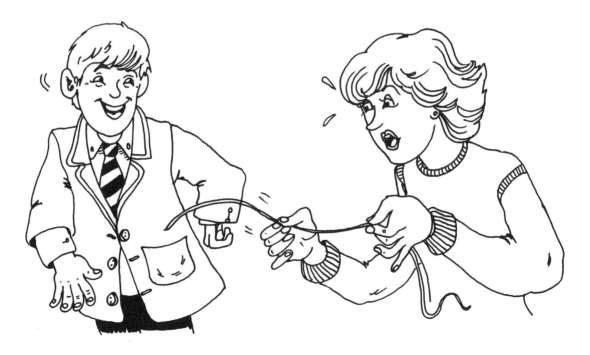

Baffling Brainteasers

On the Buses

Two bus drivers are having a cup of tea in the canteen. One bus driver is the father of the other bus driver's son. How are the two bus drivers related?

Day by Daze

When the day after tomorrow is yesterday, today will be as far from Sunday as today was from Sunday when the day before yesterday was tomorrow. What day is it?

Courtship Conundrum

The three Morgenstern sisters Magnolia, Matilda and Monica led the three Montgomery brothers Marmaduke, Maurice and Melvin a merry dance. For most of the time they could never decide who should go out with whom, and there were the most fearful rows about it. They were only sure of five things:

That Marmaduke was an accountant.

That Matilda did not go out with the doctor.

That the lorry driver's girl-friend was not Monica.

That Maurice went out with Magnolia.

That Melvin was a doctor.

Given that information, can you work out which girl was supposed to be going out with which boy?

Housey Housey

Three other sisters, Anna, Barbara and Clara Higginbottom, bought themselves a house. It cost £50,000.

If Anna had borrowed a third of Barbara's money, and half of Clara's, she could have bought the house by herself.

If Barbara had borrowed half of Anna's money and a quarter of Clara's, *she* could have bought the house by herself.

And if Clara had borrowed a quarter of Anna's money and one-sixth of Barbara's, *she* could have bought the house by herself.

How much money did each sister have in the first place?

Broad Acres

When Sir Septimus Silage died, his 647,100-acre mixed arable and dairy farm was to be divided between his three sons, Augustus, Broderick and Cuthbert. But it was not to be divided equally. Oh no. Sir Septimus had liked his sons in inverse proportion to their age, so he willed that the land should be divided so that for every 500 acres Augustus, the first son, received, Broderick, the second son, would get 600 and Cuthbert, the third son, 700. How many acres did each son inherit?

Age of Discretion

When young Amelia Jane asked her mother how old she was, she received the reply: 'Your age is now a quarter of mine, but five years ago it was only one seventh.'
    How old are Amelia Jane and her mother?

Shopping Spree

Hiram B. Hackleheimer III was on holiday in London with his wife Lulubelle and their young son Hank B. Junior. They visited a large toyshop in the centre of the city, and Hiram B. gave Hank B. Junior a sum of money to spend. Hank B. Junior gave a whoop of joy, and rushed round the shop looking at all the wonderful things he could buy. In the end, this is how he spent his money.

    One-tenth went on computer games.

    Four-ninths of what remained went on sports equipment.

    One-tenth of the remainder went on an Action Man.

    Two-ninths of the remainder went on an electronic football.

    Four sevenths of the remainder went on a game.

    Two-thirds of the remainder went on a calculator.

    Forty-nine-fiftieths of the remainder went on a book.

    Four-fifths of the remainder went on sweets (or candy, as Hank B. Junior called it).

    When Hank B. Junior had bought all his purchases he had exactly one penny left. How much money had his father given him in the first place?

Postal Puzzle

While Hiram B. was in London he decided to buy some stamps so he could send postcards home. Unfortunately he was very ignorant of the cost of stamps in Britain. He went to the post office with a £1 coin and asked for the following.

'Some 2p stamps, please, ten times as many 1p stamps, and whatever is left out of the pound please give me in 5p stamps.'

How many stamps did he buy at each price, and how many stamps altogether did he receive?

Pinta Puzzle

If you want to measure out exactly one pint of water, and you have only a three-pint jug and a five-pint jug, how would you do it?

Office Task

A secretary is given the job of clearing out some old files. She manages to clear 100 in one working week, i.e. five days. She started rather slowly, but picked up speed, so that each day she managed to clear six more files than on the previous day. How many files does she clear in each of the five days?

Typing Pool

The eleven girls in Smithson's typing pool had all been trying hard to save money for their holidays. Some of them were much better at it than others. If you were told the following facts, could you work out exactly how much money each girl had saved? You should be able to!

Anna had saved four times as much as Belinda

who had saved £85 more than Clara

who had saved £6 less than Doreen

who had saved £9 less than Ethel

who had saved £12 more than Freda

who had saved £282 less than Gloria

who had saved £283 more than Harriet

who had saved £2 more than Isobel

who had saved £135 less than Jenny

who had saved twice as much as Kerry

who had saved £1066 short of the total of all the girls' savings!

Ball Games Beano

Crockey

As you may gather by its name, this game is a cross between golf and hockey. To play it you need a hockey stick, a golf club, or a walking stick, and a plastic lemon which has been filled with water. This forms your 'ball'. You can play with an ordinary ball, but you will find it easier with a lemon.

Before you can play you need to mark out a course consisting of at least nine 'holes' and a number of 'bunkers'. The holes can be marked on a lawn by small sticks pushed into the ground, or on a hard surface by stones or chalk marks. The holes should be numbered from 1 to 9.

Along the course you need to construct a number of bunkers, between six and eight would be a good number. The bunkers can be made from bricks, boxes, flowerpots, pieces of wood laid flat to act as barriers, pairs of sticks laid flat to make a passageway, and so on.

The game is started by driving off from a starting 'tee' near the first hole. The aim is to drive the lemon to the first hole, second hole, and so on to the ninth, without touching it, avoiding the bunkers on the way, in the fewest possible number of strokes. Each player counts the number of strokes they make, and the one with the smallest number is the winner.

Bounce in the Bucket

For this game you need an ordinary household bucket and a tennis ball, or similar ball that will bounce.

The bucket should be propped on its side with the lowest point of its rim about 12cm (5 in) above the ground. You can use sand, stones, bricks or soil to hold the bucket in position. About two metres in front of the bucket, draw a line, or mark a line with a stick or rope.

Each player stands behind the two-metre line and tries to throw the ball from there in such a way that it bounces into the bucket and remains inside. It is not easy to do, and each player is allowed three goes. The player who gets the ball in the bucket the greatest number of times with the fewest number of throws is the winner.

Ball Statues

This is an amusing game that can be played at parties.

Players stand round in a circle and throw the ball round from one to another. Anyone who drops the ball has to 'freeze' like a statue in the exact position in which they are when they drop the ball, and stay like that until the end of the game.

As the game progresses there are more and more frozen statues, often in very amusing positions, and all the players have an enjoyable time whether they win or lose.

Dodge Ball

This is a good game to play on a beach, but it can equally well be played in a garden or park. It needs ten or more players, and a large, soft ball, such as an inflatable beach ball.

All the players except one stand round in a large ring. The single player, who is called the Dodger, stands in the centre of the circle.

The idea is for the player in the circle with the ball to throw it at the Dodger, on the word 'go', aiming to hit him below the waist with it. The Dodger dodges about to try and avoid being hit. Players in the circle must not move their feet, so if the ball does not hit the Dodger the nearest player to the ball should pick it up and have another go. Or the Dodger can pick up the ball and throw it to anyone they like to restart the game.

The game is best if played fast and furiously, so players have to be ready to retrieve the ball and throw it at the Dodger as quickly as possible. If a player hits the Dodger he or she changes places with him.

___

French Cricket

The number of players in French cricket is not important, but it is best to have between four

and six. One is the batsman, one the bowler, and the rest are fielders.

The ball should not be too hard or too bouncy, so it will not damage either the batsman or anyone's windows. A small cricket bat can be used as the bat, or a rounders bat, a cricket stump or a tennis racket.

The aim of the bowler is to get the batsman out, which is achieved by hitting the batsman on the leg below the knee, or by a fielder catching the ball the batsman has hit before it touches the ground. The batsman is also out if he moves his feet.

It is the batsman's job to hit the ball, and prevent it from hitting him. He does not run, but 'runs' can be scored by good hits. Scores should be agreed beforehand — say, two for balls hit to the side of the lawn, four for balls hit right to the end of the lawn, and so on. If a fielder moves his feet after touching the ball instead of throwing it straight back to the bowler it is called a 'no ball' and the batsman receives one point. Similarly if two or more fielders touch each other when trying to retrieve a hit ball, a no ball is scored.

Each player has a go at batting — there are no teams as such — and the batsman with the highest score wins.

Calculator Games

The Leaping Eight

This is a trick you can practise on your own before amazing your friends with it.

Multiply 205128 by 4. Then divide the answer by 4. Keep doing this, first multiplying and then dividing and see what happens. The 8 leaps from the front of the row of digits to the back, and then to the front again.

Crazy Calculations

Now try this little trick. Work out the following calculations and see what answers you get.

$$1 \times 9 + 2 =$$
$$12 \times 9 + 3 =$$
$$123 \times 9 + 4 =$$
$$1234 \times 9 + 5 =$$
$$12345 \times 9 + 6 =$$
$$123456 \times 9 + 7 =$$
$$1234567 \times 9 + 8 =$$
$$12345678 \times 9 + 9 =$$

It's pretty amazing, isn't it?

Twenty-one

This is a game for two players, who between them need one calculator, two pencils and two pieces of paper.

Toss a coin to see who is to start. The first player then chooses any number from 1 to 9, presses the key on the calculator and writes the number down on his or her piece of paper.

The second player then presses the + sign on the calculator and adds a number of his or her choice, writing that number down on his or her piece of paper.

The first player then adds another number, but it must be one that has not been used before. (This is why numbers are written down, so players can check what has gone before.) The game continues in this way, the aim of each player being to reach a score of exactly 21, and/or to push the opponent's score over 21. If a player scores 21 then he or she wins outright; if the score is pushed over 21 then he or she loses outright. Try playing for ten rounds to see who wins the greater number of games.

Snakes and Ladders

This calculator game can be played by either two people or one. Its object is to reduce any number up to six digits to 1 by either multiplying and adding, or by dividing. This is how you play.

Enter a number into your calculator. If the number is an odd one, multiply it by 3 and add 1. If it is an even one, divide it by 2. With each answer, treat it in the same way, and see how many goes it takes to get your number down to 1.

For example, if your number was 22.

It is an even number, so it is divided by 2.	2 | 22
	11
11 is an odd number, so multiply by 3 and add 1.	x 3
	33
	+ 1
Divide by 2.	2 | 34
	17
Multiply by 3 and add 1.	x 3
	51
	+ 1
Divide by 2.	2 | 52
Divide by 2.	2 | 26
	13
Multiply by 3 and add 1.	x 3
	39
	+ 1
Divide by 2.	2 | 40
Divide by 2.	2 | 20
Divide by 2.	2 | 10
	5
Multiply by 3 and add 1.	x 3
	15
	+ 1
Divide by 2.	2 | 16
Divide by 2.	2 | 8
Divide by 2.	2 | 4
Divide by 2.	2 | 2
	1

With this number it has been achieved in fifteen goes. If two players take part, the winner is the one who finishes first.

Middle Man

This is a game for three players, who will need a calculator each. They will also need one sheet of paper and one pencil.

The aim of the game is to produce a final total which falls between that of the two other players, and this is how you go about it. Each player starts by writing a number between 1 and 15 on the sheet of paper. All the players then study the three numbers, and decide how best to produce a total with them that will fall between those of the other two players using just two mathematical functions (i.e. two of these: $+$, $-$, $\times$, $\div$). The three numbers can be used in any order, and the skill lies in trying to predict what totals the other two players will produce.

For example, the three numbers on the paper might be 5, 8, 12. Player A might decide to arrange them like this:

$$\begin{array}{r} 8 \\ -\ 5 \\ \hline 3 \times 12 = 36 \end{array}$$

Player B might do this:

$$\begin{array}{r} 12 \\ -\ 8 \\ \hline 4 \times 5 = 20 \end{array}$$

And Player C might do this:

$$\begin{array}{r} 5 \\ +\ 12 \\ \hline 17 + 8 = 25 \end{array}$$

In which case Player C wins. The first player to be Middle Man ten times is the overall winner of the game.

The Magic Seven

The number 7 has always been considered to have magical powers. In this trick, you can prove its magical qualities, for if you carry out the calculations listed below, the answer will always be 7. Try the trick on a friend.

Give your friend the calculator and tell him or her to enter any number into the calculator and also to write it down on a piece of paper. The number should be at least one digit less than the number of digits that can be shown on the calculator screen.

Tell your friend to multiply the number on the calculator by 2.

Tell him or her to add 5.

Tell him or her to add 12.

Tell him or her to subtract 3.

Tell him or her to divide the answer by 2.

Tell him or her to subtract the number entered first, which is written on the piece of paper.

And the answer will be 7!

Calculator Talk

Calculator Talk

Everyone knows that calculators are very useful little machines, but did you know you could teach one to talk? If you don't believe me, divide 7734 by 10,000, hold your calculator upside down and see what it says. You can give your calculator a name, or maybe it already has one of its own. Try entering 31573 and turning it upside down to see what your calculator is called. And if you want to tell it a joke, enter 379919 to see what its reaction is.

You can have lots of fun with your talking calculator, even though it can only say certain letters of the alphabet. These are the letters it can produce, and how to make them.

B = 8
E = 3
G (small g) = 6, capital G = 9
H = 4
I = 1
L = 7
O = 0
S = 5
Z = 2

You have to enter the numbers in the reverse order to get the letters the right way round, and, as you have seen, you have to hold the calculator upside down.

Try asking your calculator the following questions and seeing what its answer is. The numbers to press are given at the end of each question.

1. What do you like for breakfast? (993)
2. What do you wear when you eat it? (818)
3. What's your favourite musical instrument? (3080)
4. What do you say when it's time for school? (0.04008)
5. What does school make you feel? (771)
6. Who's your best friend? (317718)

Crossword Corner

You will find crosswords in other parts of the book, too, but those in this section have been chosen because they are special. They are graded in difficulty; so beginners should start at the beginning, and hardened addicts will enjoy pitting their wits against those at the end.

Beginners' Luck

Across

2. A yellow fruit (6).
4. What the sound travels along in a telephone (4).
5. You can write with these (4).
6. A vegetable which may be boiled, mashed, fried or baked (6).
10. A tool for chopping wood (3).
11. With which to clean the floor (3).
12. It goes with a bow (5).
13. Vegetable to eat with boiled beef (7).

Down

1. Instrument for taking photographs (6).
2. Your body contains many of these (4).
3. In which to read the news (9).
7. Type of cattle used to pull carts (2).
8. In which to make a favourite drink (6).
9. You might eat these with the favourite drink (5).
11. There were three blind ones (4).

Animal Magic

Across

1. Animal used for herding sheep (3).
5. In *Peter Pan*, one of these creatures swallowed a clock (9).
8. A large monkey (3).
9. A young butterfly (11).
11. Americans call him a cottontail (6).
14. This unlikely animal won a race with a hare (8).
16. Animal used for riding (5).
17. Animal that lives in the sea and eats fish (4).

Down

1. A bird that dabbles in ponds (4).
2. A creature not known for its speed! (5).
3. Large mammal with big ears (8).
4. This creature has smart black and white stripes (5).
6. Sea creature that walks sideways (4).
7. Santa's sleigh is pulled by these (4).
10. Similar to 6 Down, but larger (7).
12. Large bird eaten at Christmas (6).
13. Might be chased by a cat (5).
15. Legless reptile (5).

T-Time

Each answer in this T-shaped puzzle contains two Ts, except one that contains three!

Across
1. A badger's burrow (4).
5. Someone who is being treated in hospital (7).
7. A fish-eating member of the weasel family (5).
8. Lands owned by someone (7).
9. Give someone a nice surprise (5).
10. Run gently (4).
11. An ermine in its brown summer coat (5).
13. An unkind nickname for an overweight person (5)
14. The opposite of 'finish' (5)

Down
1. Well-built, fat (5).
2. The name of a book, for example (5).
3. The man in charge of Waterloo, for example (13).
4. Camp-site dwellings (5).
5. Nice looking (6).
6. An exam (4).
12. Eaten at breakfast or tea (5).

Ooooooooo!

The letter O appears at least twice in each answer to this puzzle, and is the only vowel used.

Across
2. What to say to a goose? (3).
4. : (5).
5. Black substance in a chimney (4).
8. Large South American vulture (6).
10. A little corner (4).
11. Short form of 'Oxfordshire' (4).
13. Being pulled along by another vehicle (2, 3)
16. It waxes and wanes monthly (4).
17. As well (3)
18. A wise Biblical king (7).
20. See you soon! (2, 4).

Down
1. Large city in Canada (7).
2. Town in the east of Britain, and in the USA (6).
3. Yoko ——— is John Lennon's widow (3)
6. Stole (4).
7. Journalist's sensational story (5).
9. Carrots, turnips and potatoes are all ——— vegetables (4).
12. Midday (4).
14. Sheep's fur (4).
15. Marco ——— was a famous explorer (4).
17. Famous Scottish golf course (5).
19. Lavatory (3).

Seek and Find

The first part of each clue in this crossword is a normal definition; the second part, in brackets, contains somewhere within it the letters of the answer in the correct order. For example, if the first part of the clue was 'Large four-legged animal' and the second part was '(They abhor seashells)' the answer would be 'horse' — they abHOR SEashells. All the answers are words of five letters.

Across
- 5. Go swimming (There's a club at Hereford).
- 6. Top room (You'll see pretty lattice-work).
- 7. Drinks container (It's used by the dog Lassie).
- 9. Waltz (Such a strange Mohammedan ceremony).
- 10. Small animal (Fresh rewards are offered).
- 12. Ugly mark (It makes your clothes tainted).
- 15. Ice-covered areas (Here some people drink soda).
- 16. Famous Russian (He has fallen into the sea).
- 17. Greeting (Sent by Ethel Longfellow).
- 18. Monstrous giants (Is their dog respectful?).

Down
- 1. Telegram (Send a taxi-cab; let's go).
- 2. Board game (It causes headaches, severe ones).
- 3. On which farm animals sleep (They're seen in famous trawlers).
- 4. Steal (Rob from a shop in Chester).
- 8. Sounds of a gun (Noises in this hot summer).
- 9. Satan (He's a hated evil-doer).
- 11. Part of the body (It's obtained during deliveries).
- 12. Talent (He's a desk illustrator).
- 13. Sound of a horse (This was nineteen eighty-five's sound).
- 14. Coalman (He takes vitamin E regularly).

Good Luck!

In this lucky charm crossword, the first letters of the across answers spell out an appropriate phrase.

Across

1. Eat nothing (4).
5. Half of twice? (4).
8. Opposite of 'lower' (5).
11. Broadcast (5).
12. Grassy areas in gardens (5).
13. St ——— is a well-known French soccer team (7).
15. Famous racecourse (5).
20. To and ——— (3).
21. Throws (5)
23. Citrus fruit (5).
24. Killer whale (4).
25. Meat from a calf (4).
26. Listener (3).
27. Colour indicating 'stop' (3).

Down

1. Wild anger (4).
2. Large monkey (3).
3. Break in two (5).
4. Drink poured from a pot (3).
6. The latest happenings (4).
7. Blackboard may stand on it (5).
9. A town on the Isle of Wight (4).
10. Quiche (4).
14. Slang for 'head' (3).
15. I am, we ——— (3).
16. River, battle in the First World War (5).
17. Something belongs to him (5).
18. Fast runner with long ears (4).
19. Like old bread (5).
20. Go by plane (3).
21. Bay (4).
22. Wound (4).

Cryptic Crossword

Beginners stop here! This puzzle, and those on the following pages, are strictly for those in the know.

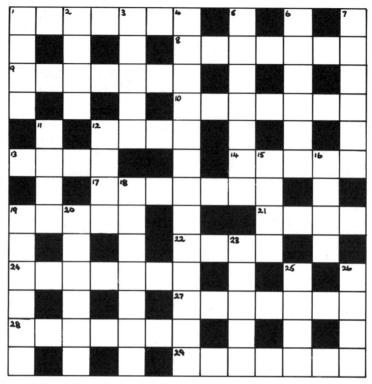

Across

1. Rover the swimmer? (5)
8. Work ... as a surgeon? (7)
9. Protective garment shows where the boss is (7).
10. I'm ordered to be in, having had a drink (7).
12. Something that's done, one way or the other (4).
13. Put your foot in it! (4)
14. Come round for a protest march (5).
17. S-supplying eggs is killing (7).
19. Sir Francis and Mr Duck (5).
21. Every peach must have its top removed (4).
22. Girl returning in readiness (4).
24. Ambassadors, for example, in funny tales (7).
27. Watch old boy send a ball on court (7).
28. A person with degree; kind of true player (7).
29. Otter in back streets stands unsteadily (7).

Down

1. Way-out do, and an alternative (4).
2. Cargoes? Car leaves ... leaves (4).
3. Annie could turn out stupid (5).
4. Drat! Oily shore could spoil this place (7, 6).
5. Recently delivered, stork style (3, 4).
6. Sounds like what a betting man will do is frolic (6).
7. Half-dead lady, in a frenzy, could prove fatal (6).
11. The cleaner shows endless charm (4).
12. Work table hidden by old Eskimos (4).
15. Editor's silver on top, old and grey (4).
16. Beat a way to eat ice-cream (4).
18. One of a pair of walkers (4, 3).
19. Everyone's unusually sad about U.S. TV series (6)
20. Sea (this one's all Greek to me) (6).
23. I sent off a little extra drawing (5).
25. Not charged, and therefore out of prison (4).
26. Enclosures for writers (4).

Against the Clock

See if you can solve this crossword in twenty minutes or less.

Across
1. The saint of Assisi (7).
9. A fruit (4).
10. A wrestling hold (6).
12. Calm the situation (7).
13. Weep or shout (3).
14. Join two pieces of metal (4).
15. A king of Troy (5).
16. Permit (3).
18. The opposite of 'attack' (7).
21. ——— -en-Provence is a town in southern France (3).
22. Whirled round (4).
24. Type of shoe sole (5).
26. Alter (5).
27. Come back to life (6).
29. A merry party-goer (8).
30. A place for storing food (6).

Down
1. Faulty (4).
2. Ready for eating (4).
3. It makes sounds louder (9).
4. Poverty (4).
5. Examine carefully (7).
6. Prophet (4).
7. Thin slice of meat for frying (8).
8. '——— old iron!' (3).
11. Great ——— is a mountain near Llandudno (4).
17. Care for (4).
19. Hearing organ (3).
20. Knowledgeable person (6).
22. Odour (5).
23. Not married (5).
24. Cut with an axe (4).
25. For ——— and a day (4).
26. '——— Maria' (3).
28. 'The Holly and the ———' (3).

Blankety Blank

Here's one to tax the brain! All the letters of the answers have been filled in, but there are no numbers to the clues or the answers, and no blanks. From the clues, work out which squares in the grid should be blacked out, and therefore what the answers should be.

S	A	W	T	F	H	W	O	R	T	H
T	E	E	R	I	C	A	L	A	R	E
A	D	D	E	R	A	R	O	V	E	R
M	S	N	A	M	E	T	V	E	E	R
P	I	E	R	C	A	M	E	N	R	A
C	K	S	I	S	T	A	R	T	H	C
F	I	D	D	L	E	R	R	M	E	T
U	O	A	S	E	N	S	N	A	R	E
D	O	Y	L	E	S	H	E	R	O	N
G	W	O	A	P	P	E	A	R	R	S
E	N	E	M	Y	D	S	T	Y	L	E

Across
Tool to cut wood
Value
Girl's name
Plural of 'is'
Viper
Common name for a dog
What you're called
Swerve
Jetty
Last word of a prayer
It twinkles at night
Violinist
Encountered
Catch in a trap
Arthur Conan ————
Wading bird
Seem
Foe
Fashion

Down
Penny Black, for instance
One of Sheffield's teams
Solid
Opposite of 'peace'
Large black bird
Oak, for example
German for 'Mr'
Bring up
Finished
Consumed
Bogs
Tired
Main person in story
Sticky sweet
Get wed
Unrelaxed
Tidy
Hit hard

Contrariwise

This is a crossword with a difference: in fact, with several differences. First of all, the answers are words that are opposite in meaning to the clues. So if a clue read 'outside', the answer would be 'indoors'. And then, if you look at the numbering of the grid, you will see something very odd. This is because the answers are not inserted from right to left, in the usual *across* fashion, nor from top to bottom, in the usual *down* manner, but from right to left (*back*), and from bottom to top (*up*). In other words, all the answers are read backwards.

Back
1. Affluent (5).
2. Helps (7).
3. Figurative (7).
4. Adorned (5).
6. Takes (5).
8. Concentrated (7).
12. Worked (6).
14. Multiply (6).
15. Health (7).
16. Sour (5).
17. Equatorial (5).
18. Success (7).
22. Lax (7).
25. Sluggish (5).

Up
5. Prose (5).
7. Relaxed (5).
8. Shallowness (5).
9. Children (6).
10. Conceal (7).
11. Darken (7).
13. Hero (7).
19. Commons (5).
20. Truly (7).
21. Attract (5).
22. Debit (6).
23. Believed (7).
24. Humility (5).
25. Accepted (7).

Catherine Wheel

In this fiendish puzzle, the answers are entered in the grid in a spiral shape. The last two or more letters of each answer form the beginning of the next one.

1. Unassuming.
2. Warship.
3. Fur.
4. Planet.
5. Notwithstanding.
6. Absolutely necessary.
7. Height.
8. Flood.
9. Japanese entertainer.
10. Disadvantage.
11. Competent.
12. Young hare.
13. Game dog.
14. Word for word.
15. Huge.
16. Signalling system.
17. American state.
18. Burdensome.
19. Person seizing power.
20. Ground that's always frozen.
21. Salary.
22. Strive.
23. Suave.
24. The drink of the gods.
25. Craftsman.
26. Firedog.
27. Wild ass.
28. Scholarly.
29. Storm.
30. Dagger.
31. Poison.
32. Blue dye.
33. Giant champion of the Philistines.

Crazy Card Games

Snap

Snap can be played by two or more people and is great fun if played fast and furiously. If more than four people play then two packs of cards are needed.

The cards should be well shuffled (the two packs shuffled together if they are used) and dealt round the players one at a time, face down, until all have been dealt. It doesn't matter if some players get an odd card more than others.

The player on the dealer's left starts by turning over his or her top card and placing it face upwards next to the pile of face-down cards. Then the player on his or her left does likewise. Play continues in this way, with each person starting a face-up pile of cards, and all the players watch intently because if two cards of the same value, i.e. two fours, or two queens, appear on two piles of cards a player can shout 'Snap!' and claim both piles of cards. If several people shout 'Snap!' then it is the player considered to have shouted first who claims the cards.

Cards won by shouting 'Snap!' are added to the bottom of the player's face-down pile and play resumes with the player to the left of the one who called 'Snap!' turning over his or her next card. If a player has used up all his or her face-down cards he or she can stay in the game provided he or she still has a face-up pile. He or she would then hope to gain more cards from a successful shout of 'Snap!'. If a player loses both piles of cards, however, he or she is out of the game.

If a player calls 'Snap!' by mistake, when two cards of the same value are not showing, then he or she has to pay a forfeit by giving one card from their face-down pile to each of the other players, who add them to the bottom of their face-down piles. The winner is the player who ends up with all the cards.

Snip-Snap-Snorem

This is a card game for three or more players with the aim of being the first player to get rid of all his or her cards.

The whole pack of cards is dealt out face down to the players, one card at a time. The players pick up their cards and look at them, but don't let the other players know what they've got.

Play starts by the person on the left of the dealer placing one of his or her cards face upwards in the centre of the table. If the next player has a card of the same value it is placed on top of the first card, with the player exclaiming 'Snip!'. If the player does not have a card of the same value, he or she says 'Pass', does not play and the next player has a turn. The next player to play a card of the value of the 'Snip!' card calls out 'Snap!', and the player who plays the fourth and last card of that value calls out 'Snorem!'. If a player has two cards of the same value in their hand they can only play one at a time when their turn comes round.

Play continues in this way until one player gets rid of all his or her cards, and thus wins the game.

Cheat

This game can be played by three or more people. It is the most fun when played with more than four players, and very exciting if played at a fast pace.

The whole pack is dealt to the players, one card at a time, face down. Each player looks at his or her cards, not letting the other players see them, and the player to the left of the dealer starts by playing one card face down on the table. As he or she plays it, the player calls out its value, which need not be its real value — hence the game's name. The next player plays a card face down and calls out its value, calling out a value above that of the previous card played. Again it may not be the correct value. The ability to cheat convincingly is part of the skill of the game!

The game continues in this way, with an ever-growing pile of cards in the centre. No player should ever let any other player see the card they are playing.

At any time a player can challenge someone who has just played a card by calling out, 'Cheat!', in which case the player has to turn up the card to show what has just been played. If the challenger is correct, and the player was cheating, then the player has to take all the cards from the central pile and add them to his or her hand. But if the player was not cheating, then the challenger has to take all the cards and add them to his or her hand. If several players call out a challenge at the same time then the challenger nearest to the left-hand side of the player being challenged is the one whose challenge is taken.

The winner is the player who gets rid of all their cards first.

My Ship Sails

This is a game for between four and seven players. Its aim is to collect seven cards of the same suit, i.e. seven hearts, seven diamonds, seven spades or seven clubs, before any other player does.

Seven cards are dealt to each player at the beginning. Any cards then left over are set aside and not used in the game. The players examine their cards, and each chooses one he or she does not want to keep, putting it face down on the table. The cards face down are passed to the left, and each player picks one up, thus gaining the card discarded by the player on their right.

Play continues in this way until one player manages to collect seven cards of the same suit. He or she then announces triumphantly, 'My ship sails!', and lays the cards face upwards on the table. This player wins the game.

Go Boom!

This game is for two or more players. Each player is dealt seven cards face down, one at a time going round all the players. The rest of the cards are placed face down in a pile in the centre of the table.

Play begins by the player on the left of the dealer playing one card and laying it face upwards beside the pile of cards. The next player to the left plays a card either of the same suit as the first card, or of the same value. For example, if the first card was the seven of clubs, then the next card must be either another club or another seven. Play continues in this way.

If a player does not have the right cards, he or she takes one from the pile face down in the centre. When all the cards in that pile have been used, the player has to say 'Pass' and miss a turn.

When each player has either played a card or passed, that is the end of the round, and the player who played the card of the highest value, with aces counting high, starts the next round. If two players have played a card of the same high value then the player who played the card first begins the next round.

The winner of the game is the first player to get rid of his or her cards, which is accompanied by a loud shout of 'Boom!'.

Dominoes

Spots Before the Eyes

Take the six lowest dominoes out of the set:
0/0, 0/1, 0/2, 1/1, 1/2, 2/2 and arrange them
in a square so that the numbers at each side of
each corner match.

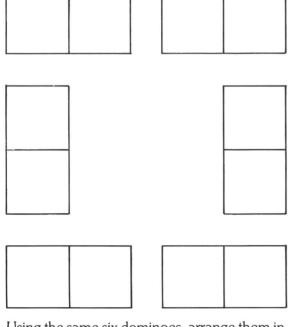

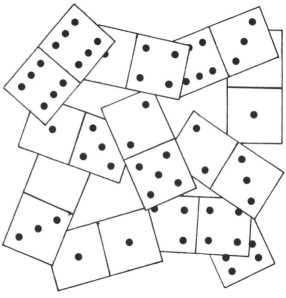

Using the same six dominoes, arrange them in
another square so that each side of the square
contains the same number of spots.

Using the same six dominoes again, form a
rectangle in which each side contains the
same number of spots.

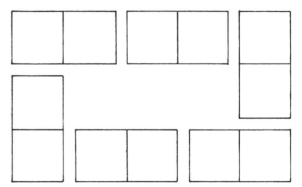

Blind Hughie

This is a simple domino game which can be played by between two and five players.

To start with, all the dominoes are placed face down on the table and shuffled around. Each player then picks up one domino to determine who shall be the lead player, the highest score on the two halves winning. The dominoes are then replaced face down on the table and shuffled round again, before the players take their dominoes. With two or three players, each takes seven; with four or five players, each draws five. The players are not allowed to look at the dominoes they have drawn, but leave them face down on the table in front of them in a row.

The player chosen to lead starts by turning over the domino at the left-hand side of his or her row and placing it in the centre of the table, face up.

The next player then looks at the domino at the left-hand side of his or her row. If it matches the piece already played, then he or she plays it. If not, it is laid face down again at the right-hand side of the row and play passes to the next player.

Play continues in this way, with each player in turn lifting the domino at the left-hand side of the row and playing it if it matches either end of the line of play, or replacing it at the right-hand side of the row if it does not. The winner is the player who gets rid of his or her dominoes first. Occasionally the game is blocked because no one can play their dominoes, in which case no one wins and the players shuffle the pieces and start again.

Dice Games

Pig

This is a dice game for two or more players and is useful if you only have one die, for that is all it requires.

Play starts with a preliminary round in which each player throws the die once in order to decide who shall begin. The player who throws the lowest number starts.

When play begins the player throws the die and scores the number it shows. He then throws again, and adds this number to his previous score. He can continue in this way for as long as he likes, until he decides to stop, or until he throws a 1. When this happens he must stop, and he loses his whole score for that turn. Play passes round the table, with each player throwing until they decide to stop or until they throw a 1. The first player to reach a score of 101 is the winner.

Round the Clock

This game is for two or more players and requires two dice. The object of the game is to roll both dice together and to score, in the correct sequence, 1, 2, 3, and so on, up to 12. For the values up to 6 either the individual die values or the combined numbers may be scored — e.g. if a three is required it may be achieved by one die showing 3 or by one showing 1 and one showing 2. After 6 the totals of the two dice are added together. The winner is the first player to reach 12.

Chicago

Chicago is a dice game for two or more players. It needs two dice, and pencils and paper for keeping score.

The game is based on all the possible scoring combinations of the two dice. It consists of eleven rounds, in each of which all the players throw the dice once, aiming to achieve the correct score for the particular round. In the first round, players try to achieve a score of 2 with the two dice; in the second round, 3; in the third round, 4, and so on. Each time a player throws the correct combination the total is added to his score. But if an incorrect combination is thrown, there is no score and the player achieves no points. The winner is the player who has the highest score at the end of the eleven rounds.

Dotty Doodles

What does each of these drawings represent?

Dotty Dots

Join up the numbered dots in the right order to see what you find!

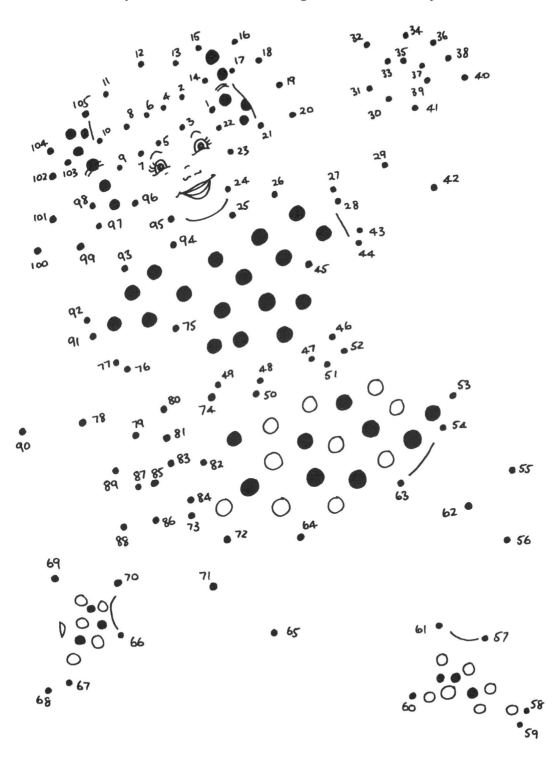

Dolls' House

How many dolls are there in this picture?

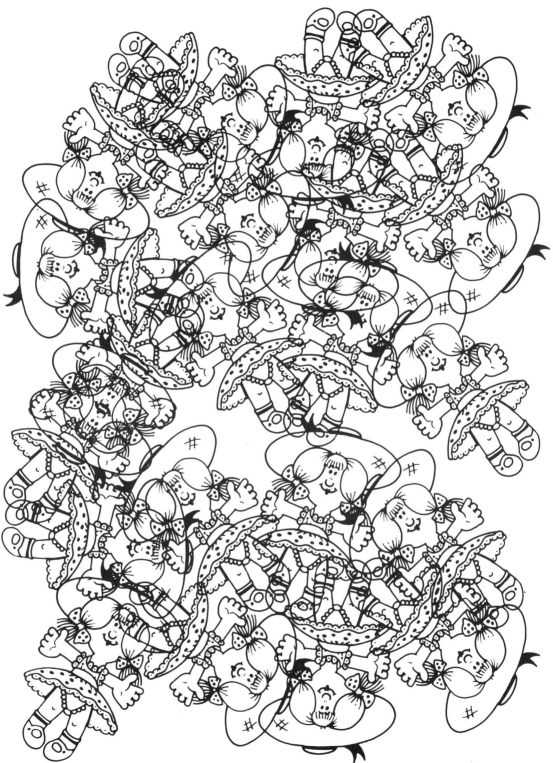

Dog House

How many dogs are there in *this* picture?

Elementary, My Dear Watson

The words, of course, are those of Sherlock Holmes, the greatest of all fictional detectives. Below is a short quiz on Sherlock Holmes and the stories that feature him, while opposite is a picture of Holmes's sitting room in which are hidden his pipe and deerstalker hat.

Sherlock Holmes Quiz

1. Who wrote the Sherlock Holmes stories?
2. Where did Sherlock Holmes live?
3. Who was his friend, helper and biographer?
4. What was the name of their landlady?
5. What musical instrument did Sherlock Holmes play?
6. Where did the great detective keep his tobacco?
7. Which was the first Sherlock Holmes book?
8. When was it published: 1867, 1878 or 1887?
9. Who was Holmes's arch enemy?
10. Where were Holmes and this enemy locked in mortal combat?

Find Holmes's Hat and Pipe

Crime at Cinderthorpe Hall

On 14 October 1897, Lord Coalscuttle, landowner and heir to the Millthorpe mining millions, was found murdered in the room marked X on the ground floor of Cinderthorpe Hall.

No one was staying at the Hall at the time, and there was no sign of a forced entry. When Holmes arrived on the scene he concluded that one of the servants must be responsible, for he knew that one of them was in the room where Lord Coalscuttle's body was found, and that he or she must have been there at the time of the murder.

From his questioning he concluded that the following statements were all true.

Harold, the handyman, was putting up new shelves in the library, which is opposite the kitchen.

Mavis, the maid, was dusting the drawing-room, which is north of the library.

Crabtree, the coachman, was waiting for his lordship in the hall.

Charlotte, the cook, was making a cake in the kitchen, which is the second room on the right as you enter the hall.

Barrington, the butler, was checking the silver in the dining-room, which is due south of the library.

Grimsditch, the gardener, was watering the plants in the conservatory.

Doreen, the daily, was vacuuming the study, which is opposite the dining-room.

Which servant was in the room with Lord Coalscuttle, and therefore was Holmes's most likely suspect?

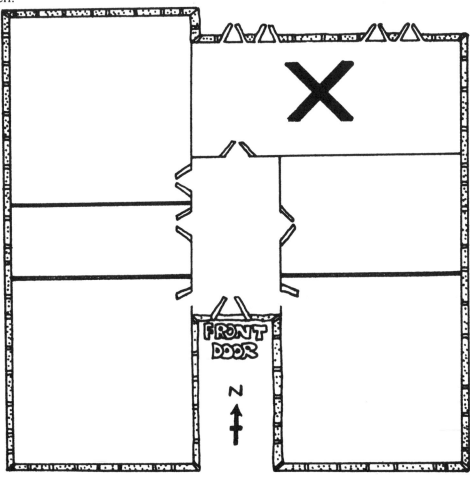

The Case of the Dalrymple Diamonds

At the time of the English Civil War, Desmond Dalrymple, the second earl, hid his family's diamonds in the garden of the Dower House, to save them from Cromwell's army.

Sir Desmond perished in the war, and the diamonds were never found. All that remained was a legend in the family that the Dower House garden should never be altered in plan, and so it never was.

Some two hundred and fifty years later, the great Sherlock Holmes was spending a few days with the Dalrymples, the current earl being his second cousin. The Dalrymple children were frequently banished to the garden, for their ceaseless chatter annoyed the detective, who wished to discuss an intriguing little problem concerning a jewel thief with their father, Sir David. One wet day, when young Davinia was playing in the cellars with her brother, Dornford (where they had both been forbidden to go), she came across a loose stone in the floor. The children scraped out some earth surrounding it and managed to haul it aside, to reveal a small cavity containing a leather folder, musty and damp. It contained a map, divided into squares, and a piece of parchment with some queer, old-fashioned writing scrawled across it.

'It looks like a map of the Dower House garden!' exclaimed Davinia, excitedly. 'But what do you suppose this means?' She waved the parchment under Dornford's nose.

'I don't know,' replied her brother, 'but I know who will! Let's go and ask Mr Holmes!'

Sure enough, when Holmes had examined the parchment, he recognized it for being a list of clues. When he had transcribed them, they read like this.

What you seek is not hidden in any area covered by the garden path.

It is not hidden at A5, nor any similar area.

It is not under the compost heap.

It is covered neither by water nor by glass.

It is not beneath any bower wherein one may sit.

It is not guarded by the dovecot.

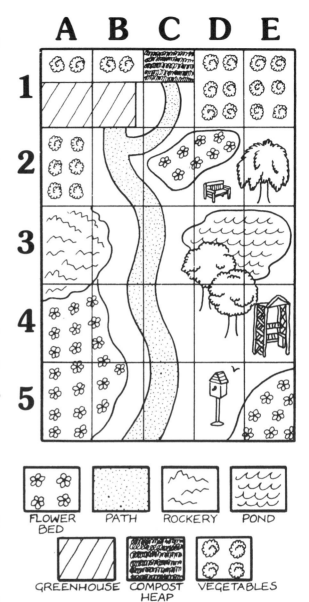

FLOWER BED   PATH   ROCKERY   POND

GREENHOUSE   COMPOST HEAP   VEGETABLES

It is not buried in any square containing a tree.

It is not hidden at A2, nor any square like it.

'By Jove, Holmes,' exclaimed Sir David, 'the clues and the map must refer to the old legend about the Dalrymple Diamonds! Come on, Davinia, come on , Dornford — we're going to do a bit of digging!'

If you were Sir David, which part of the garden would you dig up?

Evidence Enough

From the pictures you should be able to spot the clues and solve the crimes.

The Case of the Missing First Edition

THIS IS THE ROCKENHEIMER MUSEUM IN NEW YORK...

ONE OF THE MOST VALUABLE EXHIBITS IS THIS 14TH CENTURY FIRST EDITION

ONLY FOUR PEOPLE HAVE A KEY TO THE CASE...

MISS PRIM   MR DULL   MS TREND   MR DASH

ONE DAY THE CURATOR DISCOVERS THE FIRST EDITION IS MISSING!

THE CASE HASN'T BEEN FORCED - IT MUST BE AN INSIDE JOB, HANK!

WHICH OF THE FOUR KEYHOLDERS STOLE THE BOOK?

The Case of the Matron's Cheque Book

THIS IS ST. ANGELA'S HOSPITAL.

MATRON PRIM IS IN CHARGE OF THE BROKEN BONES WARD.

ON TUESDAY THERE ARE ONLY FOUR PATIENTS IN THE WARD...

AND YET MATRON FINDS THAT HER CHEQUE BOOK HAS BEEN STOLEN...

...AND SOME CHEQUES FORGED

WHODUNNIT?

'Eagle-eye' Edwards and Algernon's Alibi

After months of hard work, Detective Inspector 'Eagle-eye' Edwards of the Yard believed he had finally caught the Mayfair jewel thief, code-named 'The Cat', who had eluded both Scotland Yard and Interpol for so long. The difficulty, the inspector knew, would be pinning the crime on Algernon Algonquin, because jewel thieves of his calibre were notoriously good at arranging alibis.

Algonquin had been arrested in the early hours, when he had been found prowling in a suspicious manner round the back of Gloria Gladrags' Grosvenor Street mansion. He had said he was looking for a cufflink he had lost, and indeed was found to have one missing from his shirt, but fortunately the constable who questioned him knew his stuff and whisked him off to Scotland Yard for questioning.

It was now eight o'clock in the morning and Edwards had just come on duty. 'Let's go and see what The Cat has to say for himself,' he called to his sergeant, who was busy getting a file of papers together. 'We'll start with the last robbery — the one at Hampstead on 12 April and go backwards from there.'

Algernon Algonquin was a shortish, lithe-looking man whom Edwards thought could well shin up a drainpipe. He was well-dressed and polite, but gave no sign of nerves or guilt.

After cautioning him, Edwards said, 'We'd like a complete statement, Mr Algonquin, of what you did and where you were on the night of 12 April last between the hours 6 p.m. and midnight. Please do not omit any detail.'

'If that's the night you want to question me about then I have no worries, Inspector,' replied Algernon. 'For it was my aunt's birthday, and I travelled down to her house in Sussex in order to attend the celebrations.

'I'm very fond of my Aunt Agatha. She lives alone — she never married, you know — in a pretty little cottage with roses round the door. She likes me to go down for her birthday, as I'm her only cousin since George died.

'I set off from London at five o'clock in the evening. It was raining and the roads were slippery. As I crossed the bridge over the River Clyde I noticed the car was running out of petrol so I stopped to get some on the M5. The journey was uneventful apart from it being such a warm, dry evening that I stopped to open the car's sun roof. I suppose I must have arrived in Sussex about 5.15.

'I parked the car round the back of the block of flats and rang the bell marked "Mrs Adamson". That's Aunt Agatha, you know. Then I remembered that I'd left her present in the car and went back to get it. I'd bought her a pretty little clock for the mantelpiece, and I distinctly remember that I got it from Asprey's the previous day because I'd had to change a £25 note in order to do so. As I got the clock out of the car I noticed the time — it was 6.30.

'When I got back to her door, there was Aunt Agatha, thrilled to bits to see me. Her sister Martha seemed pleased, too. We went in and Agatha unwrapped her present. She said she'd always wanted a watch like that.

'We sat and talked about old times, and then at eight o'clock all fifteen of us sat down to a wonderful dinner she'd prepared. We had home-made soup, roast chicken, apple pie, toast and marmalade and cornflakes, with champagne to drink.

'After dinner we all played cards. Since her husband died Aunt Agatha has been particularly fond of playing cards. We played until half-past eleven, when I decided I really must leave to catch the last train back to London. I did so, and arrived back at my flat at 11.15. I put the car away, went indoors, had a hot bath and went to bed.'

'That is indeed an amazing alibi,' said Inspector Edwards. 'But I don't believe a word of it.'

Can you see why he doesn't believe Algernon? You should be able to — there are nineteen good reasons for his disbelief!

Eerie Games

Murder in the Dark

All who enjoy detective stories and excitement will thrill to this classic parlour game, which should be played by eight or more people for it to be really successful. The only equipment needed is some slips of paper and a house in which to play — the larger and creepier the better!

The slips of paper are prepared before the game is played. One is marked with a circle, one with a cross, and the rest are left blank. There should be as many slips as there are players. The slips are folded and jumbled up, and then the players each pick one. Whoever picks the circle is the detective, and he identifies himself to the other players. But the player who picks the cross is the murderer, and he says nothing.

All the lights are turned off, and the players, apart from the detective, disperse around the house. The murderer prowls around until he comes across a likely victim in a lonely place. He slinks up to the victim and whispers in their ear, 'You're dead!' The victim then screams loudly and falls to the floor, while the murderer hurries away.

When the scream is heard the other players must all remain exactly where they are, while the detective hurries to the scene of the crime, and switches on the lights. He inspects the scene of the crime, and notes down where all the suspects are. Then, in true whodunnit fashion, he summons all the suspects into the living-room where he questions them about their movements at the time of the murder.

The innocent suspects have to tell the truth, but the murderer can lie as much as he likes, unless challenged by a direct question as to his being the murderer, in which case he must confess. It is the job of the detective, by noting down what everyone says and spotting inconsistencies in their stories, to find the murderer. He is allowed two guesses after he has assembled all his evidence.

Execution

This gruesome little game is a test of the players' reflexes. It is best played by four, five or six players, and the only equipment needed is a piece of string.

One player is chosen as the executioner. He makes a running noose with the piece of string. The other players sit or stand in a circle with their forefingers raised and pressed together in the centre of the circle.

The executioner, who stands outside the circle, slips the running noose over their fingers, keeping hold of the end of the string. When he cries, 'Death!' he pulls the string tight. The cry is a signal to the players to remove their fingers as quickly as possible, for if they are caught they are out of the game. The winner is the player who remains in the longest.

Fruity Fun

Pass the Orange

This is a silly game that will make everyone laugh. You need enough players to form two teams, and two large oranges.

The first player in each team is given an orange, which he or she wedges under the chin. Once it is wedged there it must not be touched by the hands, but passed on to the next player in line, who also must not touch it with the hands. Thus the orange is passed down the line. If any player drops it, then it must be returned to the leader and the whole team starts again. Some players are much better than others, but it is a hilarious game which everyone enjoys. The first team to pass the orange successfully all along the line wins.

Fruit Machine

In this number square each fruit represents a different number. When added together, the numbers add up to the totals at the ends of the lines and columns. Work out which number each fruit stands for — all the numbers are between 1 and 6.

Lemon Trick

Can you whistle? Are you sure? Then try cutting a lemon in half and sucking half of it before you whistle. Can you still do it?

Most people can't, unless they are very used to eating lemons. This means you can play a sneaky trick with a lemon on someone else who is whistling. Just suck the lemon in

Choose just one of the bananas in the bunch and insert the needle in one of its 'seams', near the end of the fruit. Push enough of the needle in to go right across the fruit but without coming through the other side, and wiggle the needle from side to side. It will then slice through the fruit.

Repeat this at intervals along the banana, which will then be cut into neat slices all the way along its length. Hide it among the other bananas, and when anyone says they want one, offer it to them first. (It is as well to do this trick only a short while before anyone eats the fruit for otherwise it will become bruised and go bad.) The look of astonishment on the person's face when they peel the banana and discover it is already sliced will make all the preparation well worth while.

A variation on this trick is to prepare the banana beforehand and then bet someone that the next banana they eat will be ready-sliced. Of course they won't believe you, and you can have a great time proving it to them!

front of them, and you will find that because they imagine the taste in their own mouths, they will be quite unable to whistle!

Sliced Bananas

This trick will really puzzle everybody. You will need some bananas and a needle.

Fruit Picking

On this apple tree the ripe apples are shaded black, while the unripe apples are white. How many apples are ready for picking?

Fruit and Veg

This may look like an ordinary greengrocer's shop, but it contains a number of very strange things that shouldn't be there! How many of them can you spot?

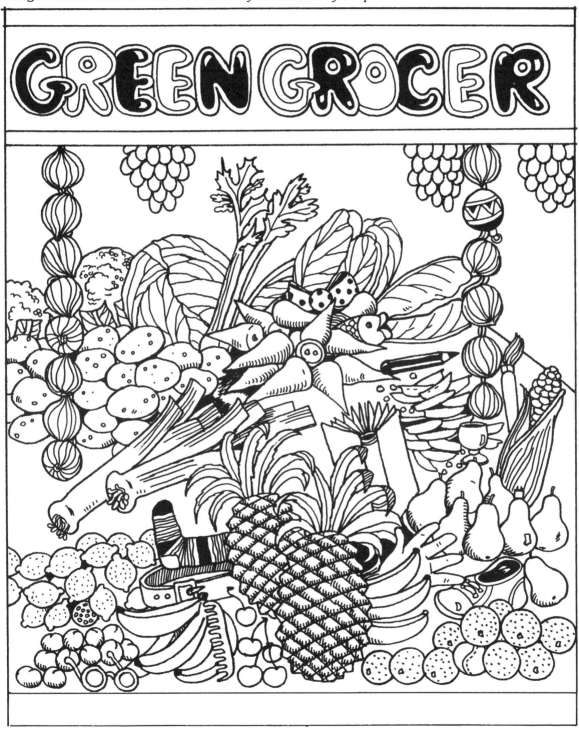

Games of Fortune

Scissors, Paper, Stone

This is an ancient game which has been played, and continues to be played, in many parts of the world. It is a game for two players.

Each player keeps one hand behind his or her back, and simultaneously they reveal the other hand in the form of scissors, paper or stone. Scissors is represented by a horizontal hand with two fingers extended, like a pair of scissors; paper is represented by a hand extended horizontally and kept flat; stone is represented by a clenched fist. Neither player knows what the other player is going to represent, and the point of the game is that as scissors cut paper, paper wraps stone, and stone blunts scissors, scissors wins over paper, paper wins over stone and stone wins over scissors. If both players choose the same shape then that round is a draw. The game continues for an agreed number of rounds, the overall winner being the player with the greater number of points.

Fan Tan

This game is a popular gambling game in China and in Chinese communities all over the world. Any number of people can play, and the game requires a board or other flat playing surface, a bowl of dried beans and a stick.

The board needs the corners marking 1, 2, 3 and 4, and in the proper gambling game each player puts a 'stake' on one of the four numbers. If you are just playing for fun, you can each choose one of those numbers, and announce to the other players which one you have chosen so there is no confusion as to who has which number.

One player is the 'banker', and he has the bowl of beans. He places a handful of the beans in the centre of the board, and with the stick he counts off the beans in groups of four. The players wait with bated breath until the last group of beans is reached, for it is the number of beans, from one to four, in the final group that the players have gambled on, or chosen, and if your number is the correct number then you win the game.

Lotto

Lotto is a game for from two to six players, and to play it you need a set of Lotto cards and numbered discs. The game is also known as Housey Housey or Tombola, and is the forerunner of the modern commercialized Bingo game.

Each player is given one of the cards, which looks like that shown below. The numbers on each card are unique to that card.

One of the players is known as the caller, and he or she has a bag of numbered discs, from which one disc at a time is drawn. As it is drawn its number is called out, and the disc is given to the player on whose card the number appears. When all the numbers on a player's card have been called he or she calls out 'Lotto' and wins the game.

Spoof

This is a game for three or more players, and it requires three small objects, such as buttons, coins, matches or paperclips for each player.

Each player puts a certain number of the objects — none, one, two or three — in their fist, holding it closed, and then holds the fist out in front of them, with the objects concealed in it. When all the players are holding out their fists, each player in turn, going round in a clockwise direction, has to guess the total number of objects concealed. Each player's guess must be different. When everyone has had a guess, the players open their fists and the objects are counted. The player who guesses correctly, or who makes the nearest guess to the correct number, wins the round.

The player who guesses first has the advantage of being able to guess any number they like, but other players have the compensating advantages that they can deduce information from the guesses already made, if they can tell when another player is bluffing.

Put and Take

Any number of people can play this game. It requires a special eight-sided top, like that in the illustration, which can be made from stiff card and marked as shown. A nail pushed through the centre allows the top to be spun.

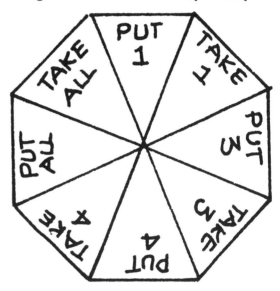

The game starts with each player putting an agreed stake into the pot (the stakes can be small coins, or buttons, counters, or any other small objects). Then each player in turn spins the top, which will come to rest on one of its eight sides, and indicate which action the player should take. The eight actions are PUT 1, TAKE 1, PUT 3, TAKE 3, PUT 4, TAKE 4, PUT ALL, TAKE ALL. These indicate the amount to be put into or taken from the pot: PUT ALL means that the player must put into the pot an equal amount to that already in there; TAKE ALL means that he or she wins the entire pot. If this happens the game is over, but if it doesn't happen the winner is the person who, after an agreed time or number of rounds, has the greatest amount of 'money'.

Globe Trotting

Capital Quiz

What are the capital cities of the following countries?

1. France.
2. Australia.
3. Ghana.
4. West Germany.
5. Pakistan.
6. Saudi Arabia.
7. Uruguay.
8. Spain.
9. Finland.
10. Nepal.

Peaks Puzzle

In which countries are the following mountains or mountain ranges?

1. Mount Snowdon.
2. Mont Blanc.
3. Table Mountain.
4. Mount Everest.
5. The Matterhorn.
6. The Pennines.
7. The Apennines.
8. The Mourne Mountains.
9. The Grampians.
10. The Atlas Mountains.

River Ripples

If you put the letters in the correct order you will discover ten famous rivers.

1. BENADU.
2. ZOMANA.
3. CALWESTERN.
4. NOJDAR.
5. TREASHUPE.
6. GOONC.
7. SENGGA.
8. ORDERGAIN.
9. BRITE.
10. THRAUBPRAMA.

Island Hopping

In which seas or oceans are the following islands?

1. Iceland.
2. Jersey.
3. Bermuda.
4. The New Hebrides.
5. The Seychelles.
6. Lindisfarne.
7. The Falklands.
8. Sardinia.
9. The Isle of Man.
10. The Isles of Scilly.

National Emblems

These animals and birds are symbols of different countries. Which countries?

Map Reading

These symbols are used on maps to identify various features. Do you know what they mean?

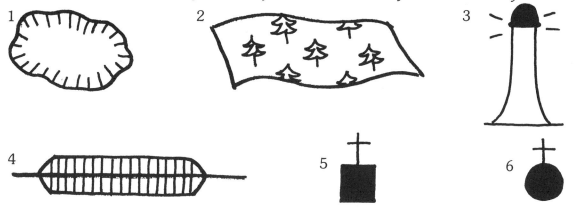

National Flags

To which countries do these flags belong?

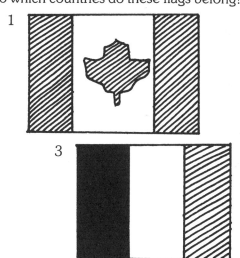

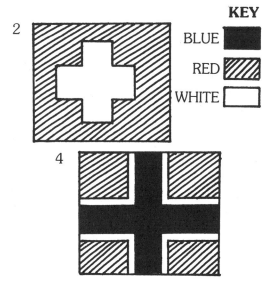

KEY

BLUE

RED

WHITE

Getting There

The distance by road from John O' Groats to Land's End is 1433 kilometres, or 891 miles. However, by the roads on this map it might be a good deal longer! See if you can find your way along them.

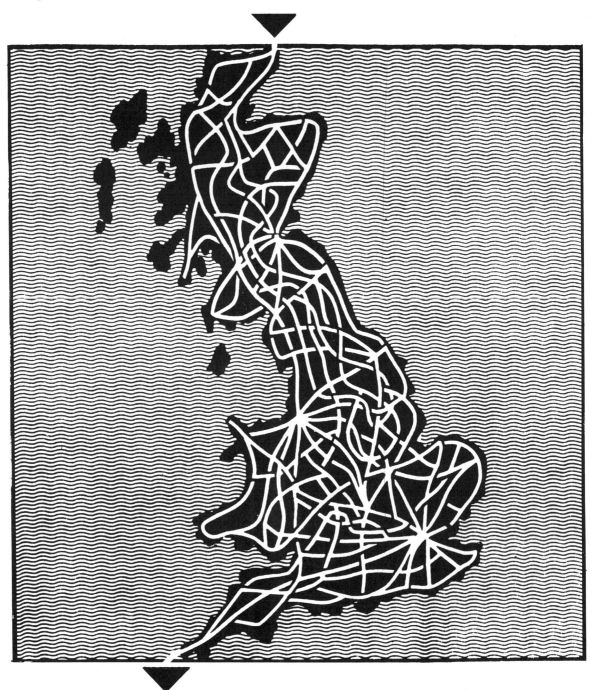

Going Places

Test your map-reading skills with this puzzle. Here is a map of part of the coast of Barnshire, together with a key to various symbols. See if you can work out the answers to the questions.

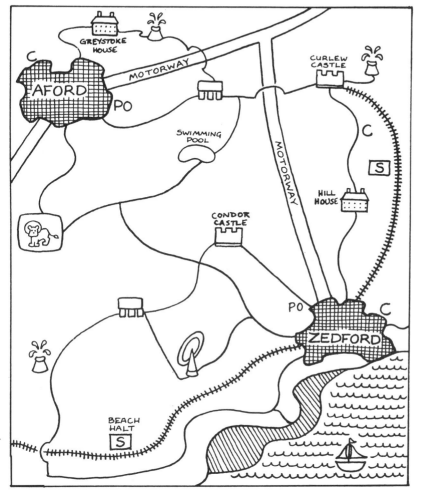

KEY

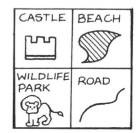

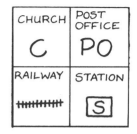

1. Which would be the quickest route by car from Aford to Zedford?

2. If, starting at Aford, you wanted to visit all the historic houses and castles in the area without travelling along the same road twice, how could you do it?

3. Could you visit any gardens without walking or travelling by bus or car?

4. If you were staying at Condor Castle, which would be your nearest church?

5. How could you travel from Greystoke House to the funfair avoiding the traffic in Aford?

6. If you were staying in Aford and wanted to go swimming, buy a postal order, visit an ancient monument, the wildlife park and the beach, what would be the shortest route you could take?

7. Is it possible to use a motorway to travel between the two ancient monuments?

8. How could you travel from Hill House to the wildlife park via an ancient monument but not a castle?

Global Games

Geography

Any number of players can play this game. Each one needs a piece of paper and a pencil.

The game can be made easy or more difficult depending on the age and knowledge of the players concerned. The idea is to take the word GEOGRAPHY, and to find the names of nine places, each of which begins with one of the letters that spell the word. If you are playing the game the easy way, these letters might include the names of countries, cities, islands or continents, such as:

G   ranada
E   thiopia
O   ran
G   lasgow
R   ome
A   thens
P   aris
H   ull
Y   ugoslavia

But if you wanted to make the game more difficult, you could say that each word has to be the name of a city, or that all the cities or countries have to be in Europe or America or Africa. The choice is yours.

Players wait until the signal to start has been given, and the first to finish the list wins.

Capital Catching

This is a children's ball game, which can be played by any number of children. They need one ball, and the presence of an adult to make sure that all the cities called out are capitals.

Players sit or stand round in a circle. One has the ball, and throws it to someone else who, as they catch it, have to name a capital city. They then throw the ball to another player, at random, who has to do the same. If anyone drops the ball, names a city that is not a capital, names one that has already been called, or fails to name one at all, then they are out. The one left catching the ball and naming a new capital is the winner.

Travellers' Tales

This is a word game for any number of players. They sit in a circle and each in turn asks two questions of the player on his or her right. In reply the first player has to name a destination beginning with the first letter of the alphabet for the first question, and a sentence of three words also beginning with A in answer to the second. Play then passes round, and the answers have to use the letter B. This is how it works.

Sally: 'Where are you going?'

Wendy: 'To America.'

Sally: 'What will you do when you get there?'

Wendy: 'Arrange apples artistically.'

Wendy: 'Where are you going?'

Ben: 'To Bermuda.'

Wendy: 'What will you do there?'

Ben: 'Braid ball baskets.'

If anyone cannot think of a suitable reply after twenty seconds then they are out. The one who stays in longest wins.

North, South, East, West

This is a game for young children. It requires the four points of the compass to be marked out in a largish room, in a garden or in a playground.

All the players group together in the centre, and an adult nominated as the caller calls out one of the four compass points. All the players then have to run to the right point. The last player to arrive calls out another compass point, and all the players run to that. The last player to arrive calls out another point, and so the game proceeds, with the players running backwards and forwards between points, and the caller being frequently changed.

Round the World Relay

This is a pencil and paper game for any equal number of players. Someone with geographical knowledge is required to check the answers, and an atlas would be useful.

The players form two teams, the first player in each being equipped with a pencil and a piece of paper. A topic is chosen, for example, 'Countries', and the first player in each team writes down the name of a country and passes the paper on to the next player. The second player has to write down the name of a country to the *west* of the first country, and he or she passes the paper on to the third player who has to write down the name of a country to the west of the second player's. Thus if the leader wants his or her team to win he or she will be careful to choose a country whose whereabouts will be known by the rest of the players. A leader who said 'Guyana' might be hard to follow.

The topic chosen could be 'Mountains', 'Rivers', 'Cities' or 'Seas', but whatever it is the rule about each successive player listing a subject to the west of that of the previous player applies. The winning team is the first to finish, provided their answers do lie to the west of each other.

General Knowledge Test

Sport Scene

1. How long is a cricket pitch?
2. Who are 'the Owls'?
3. How many hoops are used in a game of croquet?
4. What's the standard distance run in a marathon?
5. What is/are the All Blacks?
6. In which sport is the Wightman Cup played for?
7. How many points are awarded for pocketing the brown ball in snooker?
8. Which soccer team's home ground is Elland Road?
9. For which sport was Joe Louis famous?
10. What is/are the Oaks?

Animal World

1. How many humps has a Bactrian camel?
2. What do Alsatian dogs have in common with corgis?
3. Burmese, Abyssinian, Havana — what kind of animals are these?
4. Horses are measured in 'hands'. What is a 'hand'?
5. What kind of animal was a camelopard?
6. Which British mammal is known as 'brock'?
7. What is the young of a hare called?
8. What kind of animal nests in a drey?
9. Which large African animal's name means 'river horse'?
10. What kind of animal is a pipistrelle?

Famous Families

1. What were the names of the three Darling children taken to the Neverland by Peter Pan?
2. Who was the mother of Queen Elizabeth I?
3. Which famous Hungarian brothers invented the ballpoint pen?
4. Which famous French brothers pioneered balloon flight?
5. Who were the two feuding families in Shakespeare's play *Romeo and Juliet*?
6. In this acting family, father was famous for his Western roles, daughter writes health and fitness books, and son is also an actor. Who are they?
7. Whose daughter is Zara Phillips?
8. Which three famous literary sisters were brought up in a Yorkshire rectory?
9. Which two English prime ministers were father and son?
10. One brother became an actor, producer and director; the other became a naturalist and broadcaster. Who are they?

Books and Writers

1. Whose cousin was Benjamin Bunny?
2. Who created *The Snowman*?
3. Who wrote the 'Swallows and Amazons' books?
4. Who had this sign by his door?

5. Which famous fictional detective had a brother called Mycroft?
6. Who wrote *Charlie and the Chocolate Factory*?
7. Who were George, Anne, Dick, Julian and Timothy?
8. Who wrote the 'Just William' books?
9. By which number was James Bond known?
10. Which famous characters did Roger Hargreaves create?

Where in the World?

1. In which ocean is the Isle of Mauritius?
2. In which country is Trieste?
3. Where is Byrd Land?
4. Which two islands are separated by the Cook Straits?
5. Which two countries are connected by the Khyber Pass?
6. In which country is Timbukto?
7. In which country is the mouth of the River Danube?
8. Between which two countries is Baffin Island?
9. In which country is Strasbourg?
10. In which country is the Aswan Dam?

Trivia Challenge

1. What does this road sign mean?

2. What is a zloty?
3. Who was King Arthur's wife?
4. What is *son et lumière*?
5. Which Liberal MP was killed in a car accident in December 1986?
6. What are the Trossachs?
7. What was the first name of the artist Picasso?
8. Which two cities does the M5 join?
9. What is the Louvre?
10. Who was known as 'the Lady with the Lamp'?

Holiday Time

How Far?

How far are these holiday resorts from London? Distances are given first in kilometres and then in miles.

1. Aberystwyth — 280 km, 300km, 340 km / 174 miles, 186 miles, 210 miles?
2. Dubrovnik — 2350 km, 2400 km, 2450 km / 1460 miles, 1490 miles, 1522 miles?
3. Interlaken — 900 km, 925 km, 950 km / 560 miles, 575 miles, 590 miles?
4. Kendal — 400 km, 450 km, 475 km / 250 miles, 280 miles, 295 miles?
5. Nice — 1275 km, 1325 km, 1365 km / 792 miles, 823 miles, 848 miles?
6. Paris — 440 km, 460 km, 475 km / 275 miles, 286 miles, 295 miles?
7. Penzance — 450 km, 475 km, 500 km / 280 miles, 295 miles, 310 miles?
8. Rimini — 1500 km, 1525 km, 1535 km / 932 miles, 948 miles, 954 miles?
9. Rome — 1757 km, 1797 km, 1827 km / 1090 miles, 1116 miles, 1135 miles?
10. Southend — 64 km, 74 km, 84 km / 40 miles, 46 miles, 52 miles?

Airport Codes

If you fly to a holiday destination you may know that international airports have code letters by which they are known. Match the code letters in the diagram with the cities in the list.

Amsterdam
Athens
Cairo
Cape Town
Delhi
Geneva
Hong Kong
London (Heathrow)
San Francisco
Venice

Landmarks

Where in the world would you be spending your holidays if you saw these famous landmarks?

1

2

3

Foreign Phrases

What do these phrases mean, and what languages are they in?

1. Buon giorno.
2. Merci, madame.
3. Hasta la vista.
4. Guten Abend.

Shoe Shine

Shoe sizes on the Continent differ from those in England. Do you know what the equivalent would be for the following?

1. Child's size 10 in Britain.
2. Ladies' size 6 in Britain.
3. Men's size 8 in Britain.

Foreign Foods

Under each country is a list of four foods you might eat there. Do you know what each one is in English?

France	*Germany*	*Italy*	*Spain*
champignons	brot	formaggio	fresas
épinard	sauerkraut	gelato	oliva
homard	schinken	pesca	pescado
oeufs	torten	pollo	tortilla

High Life

These two pictures of Blackpool Tower may look identical, but they're not! You should be able to find ten differences between them.

Hither and Thither

In this busy holiday picture, how many people are travelling to Here-abouts and how many are travelling to There-abouts?

Holiday Crossword

All the answers in this special word and picture clue crossword are connected with seaside holidays.

Across

1. A breach in the sea wall (3).
8. Great —————— is a resort on the east coast of England (8).
11. Seagull, for example (4).
15. A hazy fog over the water (3-4).
17. Long sandy stretch by the sea (5).
18. You can drive in and spend the night here (5).

4. (5).

5. (10).

13. (10).

Down

1. You don't want these on holiday! (5).
2. It may be found in an oyster, with luck (5).
3. A resort on the north-east coast of England (6).
4. Holidaymakers hope the weather will be like this (5).
6. Someone who visits different places on holiday (7).
9. Another name for a donkey (3).
10. You may stay in it during your holiday (5).
12. A journey on a donkey at the seaside (4).
16. 'Knees bend, —————— stretch!' (4).

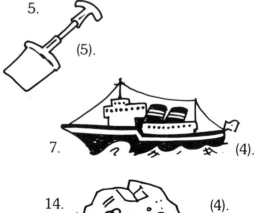

5. (5).

7. (4).

14. (4).

Holiday Resorts

All the holiday resorts listed below — from England, Ireland, Scotland and Wales — can be traced out in this word-search puzzle. Words can be read across, down or diagonally, either forwards or backwards, but always in straight lines. It may help to use a pencil and a ruler to help you find them.

AYR
BANFF
BARRY
BLACKPOOL
BOURNEMOUTH
BRIDLINGTON
BRIGHTON
BUDE
CLACTON
CROMER

DEAL
DUNBAR
FILEY
GREAT YARMOUTH
HASTINGS
HOVE
KINSALE
LOWESTOFT
MORECAMBE
NAIRN

OBAN
POOLE
RHYL
RYE
SKEGNESS
SOUTHEND
ST IVES
TENBY
WHITBY

```
E B R I D L I N G T O N
E S O U T H E N D Y E L I F
S Y U Y B T I H W E B P S T
K L R M K I N S A L E N L F
E J N N I L P E V O H D E O
G R E A T Y A R M O U T H T
N E M I B C D E H P G V F S
E M O R A B N U D K F F X E
S O U N O T C A L C N W E W
S R T S T I V E S A R D Y O
L C H Z Y R R A B L U S B L
A Y M O R E C A M B E A Z O
S Y H B R I G H T O N A L H
S R R Q S G N I T S A H
```

Holiday Games

Scavenger Hunt

Whether you're on holiday at the seaside or in the country you can have a great time on a scavenger hunt. The idea is to collect all the items listed in a set time — say a morning, a day, or even a weekend — and award yourself points for all the items you collect. In this way the hunt can either be something you do on your own, or it can be a competition with a friend to see who finishes first and who gains the greater number of points. This scavenger hunt starts with a general list that you can collect wherever you are, and then has two short lists, one specifically for seaside holidays and one for country holidays. If you are on holiday in a big city, then just collect items from the general list.

General list   *Points*

1.	A map of the area.	8
2.	The telephone number of the nearest railway station.	10
3.	A red glove.	10
4.	A local postcard.	5
5.	A photograph of Princess Diana.	7
6.	An evening newspaper.	4
7.	A 1986 penny.	3
8.	A carrier bag with the name of a local store on it.	5
9.	A green eraser.	8
10.	A purple pencil.	8
11.	A blue flower.	7
12.	A banana skin.	6
13.	A train ticket.	7
14.	An ice lolly stick.	3
15.	A spoonful of cooked potato.	10
16.	A used 26p stamp.	10

Seaside list

1.	A piece of seaweed.	4
2.	A stone with a hole through it.	10
3.	A striped shell.	8
4.	A timetable of local tides.	10

Country list

1.	A yellow flower.	4
2.	Some sheep's wool.	10
3.	A leaf off an oak tree.	8
4.	A leaflet/brochure from a place of local interest, eg. a stately home, museum, etc.	10

Pin Weed

This is a beach game for any number of players. You will need three large pieces of driftwood, or three sticks about one metre long, plus three fairly large and strong strands of seaweed.

The driftwood or sticks should be planted in the beach in a line, one in front of each other and about two metres apart. About five metres in front of these 'pins', draw a line in the sand and line up the players behind it.

Each player in turn is given the three strands of seaweed, and has to throw one strand round each 'pin'. Five points is scored for getting the weed round the first pin, ten points for getting it round the second, and fifteen for getting it round the third. At the end of an agreed number of rounds, players add up their scores and the person with the highest is the winner.

Beach Olympics

Beach olympics are an excellent way of enjoying yourself if you have a number of friends gathered together and if the weather isn't too hot. All you do is to organize a number of races on the beach. You will need to draw a starting line and a finishing line, and will need someone to stand by the latter in case there's a photo finish! Here are some ideas for races you can hold as part of your Olympics.

1. A backward race, with all the players running backwards.
2. A water race, with each player carrying a bucket of water and being disqualified if they spill any.
3. A wheelbarrow race, with the players in pairs, one of which walks on his or her hands while the other holds their legs and 'wheels' them like a barrow.
4. A three-legged race, with the players in pairs and one leg of each tied together with a handkerchief or belt.
5. A four-legged race, with the players in threes, and two lots of legs tied together.

6. A piggy-back race, with the players in pairs and one riding on the back of the other.
7. A hopping race, hopping six paces on one foot, and six on the other.
8. A head-over-heels race, with players somersaulting along the course. You may need to shorten the course for this one.

Hopscotch

Hopscotch is usually considered a school playground game, but it is ideal for the beach, especially on hard, wet sand when the tide has gone out.

Draw out the grid in the sand with a stick or your fingers. The diagram shows what it should look like. Each square should have sides 50 cm (20 in) long.

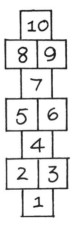

Players line up at the starting line and take it in turn to throw a pebble into one of the ten squares. If the pebble misses all the squares, or lands on a line, the turn doesn't count and the player has to go to the back of the queue. If the pebble lands in a square the player must go to that square, hopping through each single square and landing on both feet in the double squares. If, on the way, he or she lands on a line then the turn doesn't count. When he or she reaches the square containing the pebble, it is picked up and the player marks that square in a corner with his or her initials. The player then returns to the back of the queue at the starting line and awaits his or her next turn. The winner is the first player to get their initials in every one of the ten squares.

Holiday Special

Listed below are twenty popular holiday resorts and areas on the Continent. Can you match them with the numbered dots on the map?

Amsterdam	Cyprus	Lausanne	Rome
Biarritz	Dubrovnik	Monte Carlo	Salzburg
Cannes	Florence	Palermo	Sorrento
Copenhagen	Gibraltar	Paris	Venice
Crete	Ibiza	Rhodes	Vienna

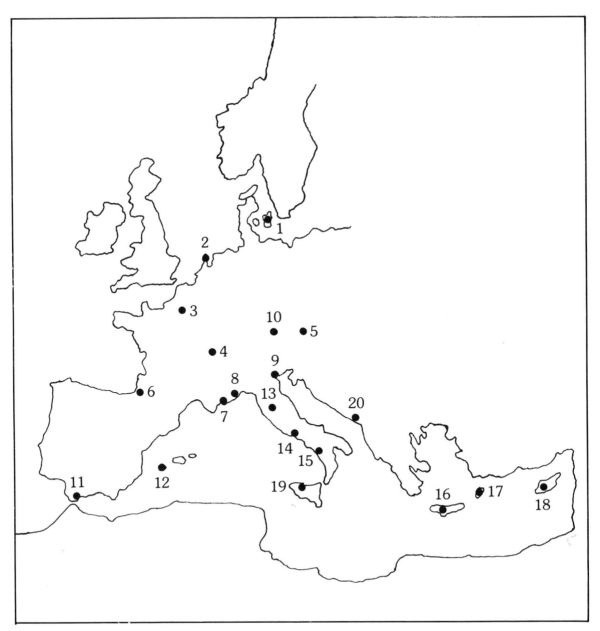

Holiday Package

Jimmy Jones is setting out for his holiday abroad. But these pictures of his preparations have been put in the wrong order. Can you put them in the right order?

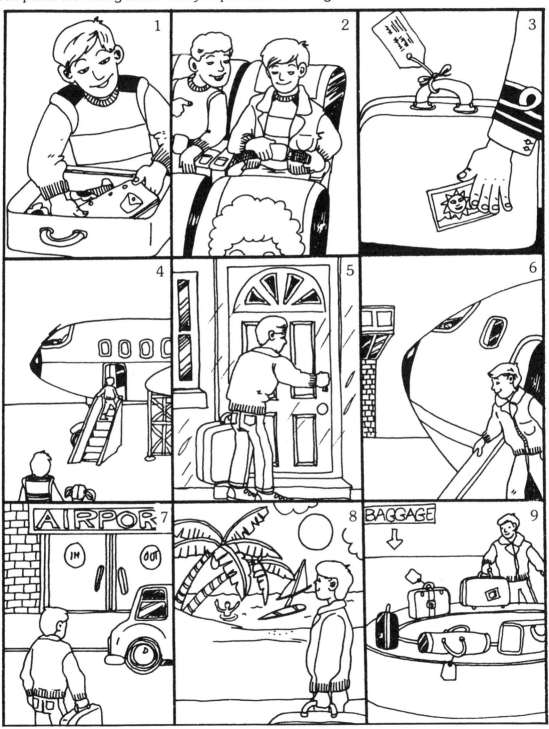

Incalculable!

Weekends Off

When asked her age, Gloria Stevvon, the former West Country beauty queen, coyly replied: 'I'm thirty-five. But that's not counting Saturdays and Sundays.' What was Gloria's real age?

One Number

If you add 1000 to a certain whole number, the result will be more than if you multiply the number by 1000. What is the number?

Driving Test

Cornelius Crankshaft drives his car a certain distance at 60 mph, and arrives at his destination one hour earlier than if he had driven at 50 mph. How far did he drive?

Soldiers

Jimmy and Johnny are playing soldiers. Jimmy shouts out to Johnny: 'Right turn! About turn! Left turn!'

If Johnny was facing due west to start with, which direction is he facing when he stops?

Vowel-less

Do you recognize this vegetable without its vowels?

NN

Potty Problem

If a flowerpot weighs 9 lb and half a flowerpot, what does a flowerpot and a half weigh?

Unlucky Thirteen

Which of the thirteen letters below does not belong to the series?

J F M A M R J J A S O N D

Art Collectors

The Ffortescue-ffyffes owned a number of valuable paintings. When asked by a reporter exactly what they *did* own, the Honourable Fiona Ffortescue-ffyffe replied, 'They're all Turners except two, all Constables except two, and all Monets except two.'

How many paintings did the Ffortescue-ffyffes own?

What's Next?

What is the next number in this series?

2   3   5   9   17   33

Er, What?

Look at the letters below. If you add three letters before them, and the same three letters after them, you can make an ordinary English word. Can you?

E R G R O

I Beg Your Pardon!

'A slight inclination of the cranium is as adequate as a spasmodic movement of one optic to an equine quadruped utterly devoid of any visionary capacity.'

What does this mean in plain English?

Truth Test

Gillie could never tell the truth. Millie could never tell a lie. One of them said, 'The other one said she is Gillie.' Which one said it?

Ninety-nine

Which number's double exceeds its half by 99?

Party Treats

Mrs Jones buys some little bags of sweets as prizes for her son Ben's birthday party. She buys a total of twenty bags, and spends £6. If the prices are 60p each for a bag of chocolates, 45p each for a bag of toffees, and 10p each for a bag of fruit gums, how many of each does she buy?

Car Cleaning

If Mrs Biggins can wash her car in ten minutes (it's only a Mini and she doesn't do it very well), and her friend Mrs Wiggins can wash it in five minutes (she does it even less well), how long would it take if they both washed the car together?

Sleepyhead

Samantha Snoozealot has overslept. She flings on her clothes and rushes downstairs, on the way seeing the reflection of the dining-room clock in the hall mirror, and nearly has a fit, for the time appears to be 2.30. What time is it really?

Jane's Jeans

Jane Jenkins bought a new pair of jeans, and, as an afterthought, a belt to go with them. She spent a total of £21, and the jeans cost £20 more than the belt. How much did the jeans and the belt cost individually?

Just Supposing

If a third of 6 were 3, what would half of 20 be?

Subtraction

How many times can you subtract the number 5 from the number 42?

Number, Please

Find a number the square of whose half is equal to the number with its digits reversed.

Leap Year

Last leap year Tracy set her alarm clock to wake her at 9 a.m. and went up to bed at eight o'clock on 29 February. If she slept soundly until the alarm clock went off, how many hours' sleep did she get?

Introducing Cryptarithmetic

In these amazing sums, letters have been substituted for numbers. Can you work out in each case what the numbers should be?

Roman Riddle

```
      V I
      V I
      V I
  +   V I
  -------
      X V
```

Find Me

```
        E
        E
  +     E
  -------
      M E
```

Scrabble

```
    L E T T E R S
  + A L P H A B E T
  ---------------
  S C R A B B L E
```

Urgent Plea

```
    S E N D
  + M O R E
  ---------
  M O N E Y
```

Fly For Your Life

```
      F L Y
      F O R
  + Y O U R
  ---------
    L I F E
```

In this sum I = 1 and O = 0.

Seamstress

$$I \times MEND = DENIM$$

Adding Up to Sixty

```
      T E N
      T E N
  + F O R T Y
  -----------
  S I X T Y
```

Adding Up to Twelve

```
        T W O
      T H R E E
  + S E V E N
  -----------
  T W E L V E
```

There are two possible solutions to this one.

Inventory

Match the scientists on the left with their inventions on the right.

1. Charles Babbage	diesel engine
2. Alexander Graham Bell	radio telegraphy
3. Christopher Cockerell	electric razor
4. Rudolf Diesel	'cats'-eyes'
5. Thomas Edison	jet engine
6. Michael Faraday	camera
7. Alexander Fleming	electric battery
8. Benjamin Franklin	balloon
9. King Camp Gillette	aeroplane
10. Johann Gutenberg	fountain pen
11. Joseph Lister	computer
12. Guglielmo Marconi	hovercraft
13. Joseph and Etienne Montgolfier	electric light
14. Joseph and Claude Niepce	telephone
15. Jacob Schick	dynamo
16. Percy Shaw	penicillin
17. Alessandro Volta	antiseptics
18. Lewis Edison Waterman	lightning conductor
19. Frank Whittle	printing
20. Wilbur and Orville Wright	safety razor

Island Heritage

How many of the islands outlined on these pages do you recognize? They are not drawn to scale, and some are much easier than others!

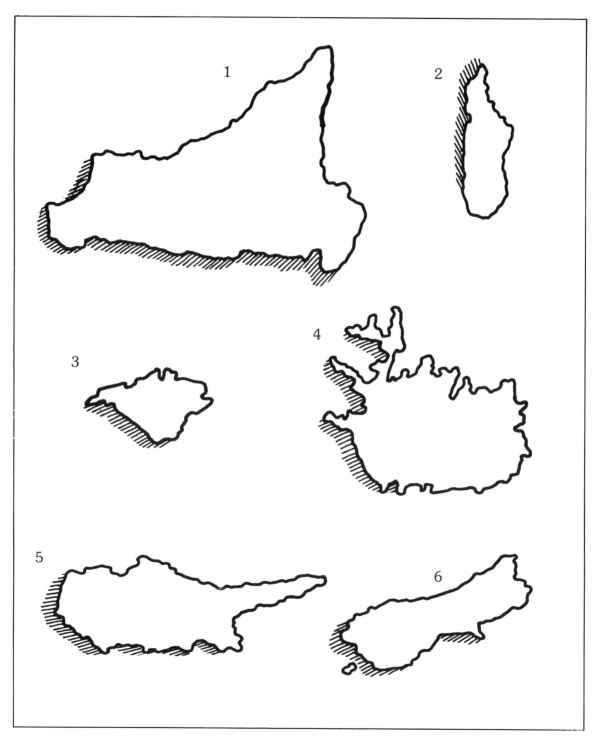

7

8

9

10

11

12

81

Incredible Impersonations

If you've ever wished you could impersonate someone, here's your chance to learn how. If you do it properly you can have a lot of fun, and it's a great way of playing a joke on someone.

Taking Notes

The first thing to do is to study the person you want to impersonate. Notice first of all their size and shape, then how they dress, walk and move about. Are they tall and straight? Short and fat? Do they have a stoop? Do they move energetically or are they more relaxed?

Then take note of how they speak. Listen to their voice. Is it high-pitched or low? Do they speak quickly or slowly? Do they wave their arms about a lot when they speak?

Finally, take very careful note of their facial expressions, the most difficult thing of all to get right. When you think you have noted everything down, spend some time practising in the privacy of your room before trying out the character in public.

Here are some tips to help you.

Physical Shape

It is difficult to make yourself look thinner, except by wearing rather large, loose clothes, but it is easy to make yourself look fatter by strapping a cushion or two under a large top coat.

You can make yourself look taller by wearing high-heeled shoes (even if you are a boy!), or shorter by stooping forward from the waist and rounding the shoulders — the way you have probably been taught not to stand or walk.

Movement

If the person you are impersonating has a limp, put a pebble in your shoe, making sure it's in the correct one, and you will automatically walk with a limp and remember which leg to limp with! To give yourself a stiff knee, tie a ruler behind your knee with a bandage. Practise moving with short, quick energetic movements, or long, slow languid ones, according to which type of person you are trying to copy.

Do they have lots of little mannerisms? They might scratch their ears when speaking, or rub their chins. Practise any little tricks like this, they will make your impersonation instantly recognizable. Are they right- or left-handed? It is important to get that right.

Dress

It can be difficult to copy someone's dress, especially if they are a glamorous sort of person, but the general effect of smart, tight clothes or loose casual ones can be aped.

Wearing a hat is a good idea because it can totally alter your appearance. It can be pulled well down to disguise you. If you have long hair you can tuck it under the hat to make it appear short. If you have short hair you can glue artificial hair, or even wool, round the edge of the hat to make it appear as if you have long hair.

Don't forget details of dress such as shoes and jewellery, and do your best to copy them. You may find lots of suitable items very cheaply in a charity shop or other secondhand shop.

Voice

Getting the voice right is very important. If you are lucky enough to have a tape recorder then you could tape the person's voice and play it over and over to study it before trying out the voice yourself. Tape your voice, too, and see if you sound at all right. If you do this you will know where you are going wrong, and can make corrections.

You can alter the sound of your own voice in a number of ways. Try speaking with your mouth in a permanent and wide grin, or placing your tongue either behind or in front of your bottom teeth, and you will sound quite different. Don't forget that you may have to make your voice sound higher or lower, or to speak more slowly and more quickly than you usually do. Don't forget, also, to notice if your character has a catchphrase, or if they are always saying 'you know', or 'like' in their ordinary speech. If so, you will have to practise incorporating the words and phrases into your own speech.

Face

You can make your face look fatter by putting pads of clean cotton wool in your cheeks and around the inside of your lips. You can lighten the colour of your skin by rubbing it with talcum powder, or darken it by rubbing it with cocoa. If you can borrow your mother's or sister's make-up you can have a wonderful time, drawing lines on your face to make yourself look older with an eye pencil. If you pucker your face into a frown you will see where the lines naturally occur, across your forehead, between the eyebrows, and running down from your nose to the corners of your mouth. You can also turn yourself into a glamorous woman by using make-up, but you might need a bit of help in applying it at first. Another easy way of changing your facial appearance is to wear spectacles, either real ones without lenses, or sunglasses.

Hair

Try changing your parting, or brushing your hair back instead of forwards, and you will be surprised how different it makes you look. If you want to look older, rub some talcum powder into your hair to give the appearance of grey.

Jingle Bells

Carol Singing

Below are a number of lines from well-known Christmas carols. Are they all quoted correctly?

1. 'Away in a manger, no crib for a bed
   The baby Lord Jesus laid down his sweet head.'
2. 'O come all ye faithful,
   Happy and triumphant.'
3. 'The holly and the ivy
   When they are both full grown,
   Of all the trees that are in the wood
   The holly wears the crown.'
4. 'God rest you merry, gentlefolk,
   Let nothing you dismay.'
5. 'Hark! The herald angels sing
   "Glory to the new-born King,
   Peace on earth and mercy mild
   Christ and sinners reconciled!"'
6. 'It came upon the midnight clear
   That joyful song of old.'

True or False?

How many of these statements about Christmas are true?

1. Christmas is derived from the ancient Roman festival called Saturnalia.
2. St Nicholas's Day is 16 December.
3. Christmas Day used to be celebrated on 6 January.
4. At midnight on Christmas Eve farm animals are said to gain the power of speech.
5. It is considered unlucky to be born on Christmas Day.
6. Italian children traditionally received their Christmas presents on 6 January from a friendly witch called La Befana.
7. *A Christmas Carol* is a famous book by John Bunyan.
8. Holly is said to have the power to ward off various illnesses.
9. Mistletoe is often used to decorate churches at Christmas.
10. Christmas decorations should be taken down by 12 January.

Christmas Hits

Match these singers/groups with their Christmas hit titles. Some of them were hits quite a long time ago, and some songs were recorded by more than one artiste.

'Blue Christmas'
'Christmas Alphabet'
'Little Drummer Boy'
'Make a Daft Noise For Christmas'
'Mary's Boy Child'
'Merry Christmas Everybody'
'When a Child is Born'
'White Christmas'
'Wonderful Christmastime'

Jolly Christmas Junkets

Merry Christmas and a Happy New Year

This is a verbal game that will be enjoyed by everybody. Any number of people can play, and all they need is to be able to do simple arithmetic.

Players sit round in a circle and count in turn from one to infinity, with each player saying a different number. But the numbers five, seven and multiples of five and seven must not be mentioned. Instead of five or its multiples, players must say, 'Merry Christmas'. And instead of seven and its multiples, they must say, 'A Happy New Year'. Any number which is a multiple of both five and seven is replaced by saying, 'Merry Christmas and a Happy New Year'. This is how it works up to twenty-one.

One

Two

Three

Four

Merry Christmas

Six

A Happy New Year

Eight

Nine

Merry Christmas

Eleven

Twelve

Thirteen

A Happy New Year

Merry Christmas

Sixteen

Seventeen

Eighteen

Nineteen

Merry Christmas

A Happy New Year

Any player who says the forbidden numbers, or 'Merry Christmas' when they should have said 'A Happy New Year', or vice versa, drops out. The winner is the last player left in counting, and to make the game both amusing and exciting it should be played fast and furiously.

Blind Man's Buff

One of the oldest and most popular of party games, Blind Man's Buff has been played in different parts of the world for more than 2000 years. You need four or more players and a blindfold.

If you want to play the game in the traditional way, you stand the player chosen as the 'blind man' in the centre of the room and cover his or her eyes with a blindfold. The other players then say to the blind man, 'How many horses has your father got?'

He or she replies, 'Three.'

The other players ask, 'What colours are they?'

The blind man replies, 'Black, white and grey.'

The other players chant, 'Turn round three times and catch whom you may.'

The blind man then revolves three times and tries to catch one of the other players, all of whom rush out of his way. When one of the players is caught, he or she becomes the blind man for the next round. You should make sure, before playing the game, that there is nothing in the room that the blind man might trip over, or knock over and break.

Ankle Peeping

In Victorian times this game would have been considered extremely daring! Players form two teams, one of which leaves the room while the other removes their shoes and socks, stockings or tights. This team lies on the floor in a row, and covers themselves, apart from their feet and ankles, with a large sheet. When the other team returns, their task is to guess which feet belong to which person. It is surprising how many people who are close to each other don't recognize each other by the feet and ankles alone! When everyone has made their guesses, the teams change over. The team who has the most correct guesses wins.

Charades

This is also a team game for two teams, each of which can contain any number of players. Each team has to think of a word of two or three syllables which can be acted out in front of the other team, who has to guess what the word is.

Each syllable is acted out separately, and then the whole word is acted out. For this reason it is as well to be careful about the choice of words. Good ones are words like seaside, armchair, football, snowman, raincoat, pencil, etc.

Let us suppose 'snowman' is chosen as the word. First of all, the team has to act out the word 'snow'. In all the acting no words must be spoken. Snow might be indicated by people digging and sweeping, by skiing, sledging, and so on. A few minutes should be allowed for each word to be guessed. The second part of the word, 'man', is more difficult to act. But it might be indicated by miming masculine jobs, like brick-laying, lorry-driving, and so on, with the emphasis on strength, making much show of feeling the biceps muscles in the arm. Finally the whole word is acted out. People should again shovel snow, roll it into a big ball, pat it into place, mark out imaginary facial features, buttons, and so on.

When one team has finished acting their word, if the other team has guessed it correctly, they take their turn to choose and act out a word. If they have not guessed it, the first team can have another go.

Jumbled Christmas Boxes

The four squares in the top left-hand corner of the grid are repeated together in the same pattern just once elsewhere in the grid. Can you spot where?

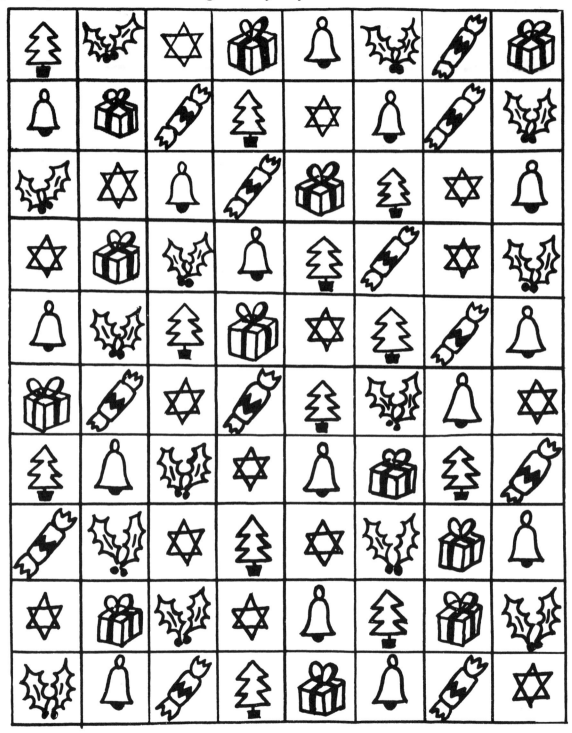

January Jaunt

One of these six pictures contains something from each of the other five. Which one is it?

January Brings...

Snowstorm

Every snowflake that falls is different from every other snowflake, but on this page there are two that are identical. Can you spot which two?

90

Snowman

Can you find your way through this snowman maze? Start at the top arrow and finish at the side arrow.

First Steps in Juggling

Have you ever wished you could juggle? Here's your chance to learn. On these pages you will find six steps to learning how to do it. If you practise hard you will soon become proficient. Juggling is best performed with a fairly heavy, solid rubber ball.

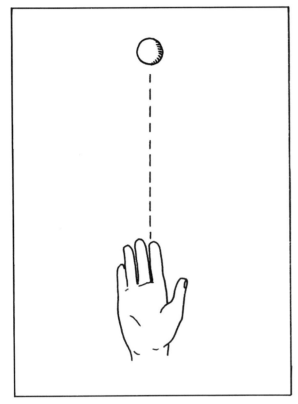

The Vertical Fall

This is the first step to master. The idea is to throw the ball up into the air vertically so that it lands in the same spot as that from which it was thrown. The hand doing the throwing should move as little as possible. It sounds easy but if you've never done it before, you may be surprised! Practise with both hands until you can do it with either, with your eyes closed.

The Horizontal Pass

This simply means throwing the ball from one hand to another as quickly as possible, and in as near a horizontal line as possible. As your skill improves, move your hands further apart.

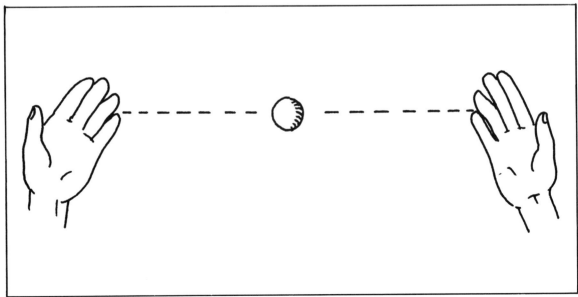

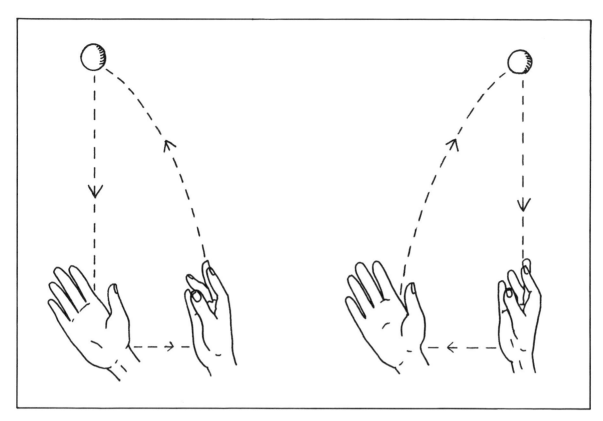

The Inside Fall and Outside Fall

Hold the ball in your right hand and throw it in such a way that it travels in an arc and then drops down to your left hand. But instead of catching it in your left hand, quickly move your right hand across to catch it. Then, keeping your right hand in that position, throw it back in the same way, but this time from left to right, moving your right hand back to its original position to catch it.

Practise this trick with both hands until you can perform it equally well with either.

Falls From Right to Left

These are similar to the movement above, but both hands are used. Throw the ball from the right hand so that it falls to the left. Catch it in the left hand and throw it towards the right, and catch it with the right hand. Practise until you can do it quickly and efficiently.

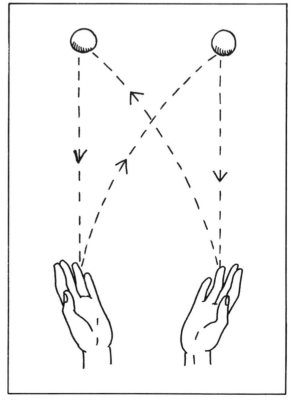

The Double Inside Fall

This is similar to the Inside Fall and Outside Fall, except that two hands are used at the same time and two balls are kept in motion. Start with a ball in each hand. Throw the one in the right hand towards the left, and before it has reached the left hand throw the other ball from the left hand to the right. To stop the balls colliding throw one slightly higher than the other. If you time it properly it should be possible to keep the two balls in motion, though it takes a bit of practise.

The Simple Shower

This trick keeps two balls in perpetual motion moving round in the same direction. Start with a ball in each hand, and throw the right one in the air towards the left. While it is in the air, transfer the the ball in the left hand to the right using the Horizontal Pass. This ball is then thrown up in the air again from right to left. Practise doing the trick both clockwise and anti-clockwise.

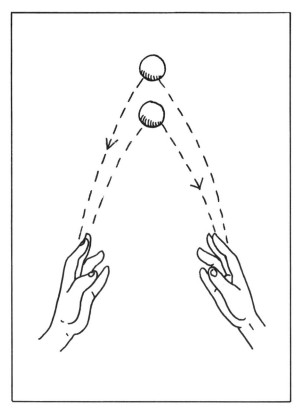

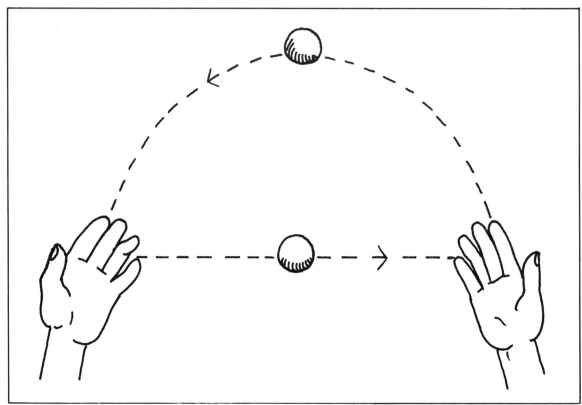

Jumpers and Boots

The pictures are all clues to words that can be filled in in the Across squares on the grid. If you get them all correct, you will find that the arrowed column spells out another source of winter warmth reading down.

Kids' Stuff

This is a specially easy section for younger members of the family.

Pocket Money

Sally and Simon have each been given £1.50 pocket money. They decide to spend most of it on sweets. This is what Sally buys:

- 2 lollipops at 20p each
- 1 bar of chocolate at 35p
- 1 bag of peppermints at 45p
- 1 bag of sherbet at 17p

How much has she spent, and how much money does she have left out of her £1.50?

This is what Simon buys:

- 1 ice-cream at 30p
- 1 toffee bar at 19p
- 1 bag of fruit drops at 35p
- 2 fruit chews at 12p each

How much has Simon spent, and how much money does he have left out of his £1.50?

Bag of Goodies

These are some of the sweets Sally and Simon saw in the shop. How many different kinds are there in the bag?

Rhyme Time

There are ten pairs of objects that rhyme pictured here. Can you spot them all?

Crossed Wires

Andrew, Ben and Chrissy have got their Walkman wires crossed! Which Walkman belongs to which child?

Trouble Decker

There are a lot of naughty children and animals on this school bus. Can you find ten differences between the two pictures of it?

Space Chase

This is a fantastic space-race game for two or more players. Open the book out flat and play it as you would any other board game, with a die, something to shake it in, and counters (or coins, buttons, etc.) for each player.

The Earthling (you) is on enemy territory on Planet X13, and wants to get back to his spaceship on square 64 as fast as possible, avoiding all the hazards on the way. Throw a six to start, and then have another throw to see which square you should travel to. There are no extra throws for sixes during the game. The first player to land on square 64 wins.

101

Crazy Maypole

There are ten deliberate mistakes in this dancing-round-the-Maypole picture. Can you spot them all?

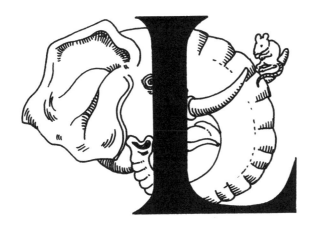

Ladder Words

By changing one letter at a time, the word BOOT can be turned into the word SHOE like this:

B	O	O	T
S	O	O	T
S	H	O	T
S	H	O	E

Now see if you can turn HEAD into TAIL, FOUR into FIVE, and RICH into POOR.

Likes and Dislikes

This game has a leader, whose job it is to say aloud what it is he likes and dislikes. But they are not just a random selection of things. Before he speaks he has to think of some kind of reasoning behind his choice. For example, he might say:

I like bees but I don't like wasps.

I like butterflies but I don't like moths.

I like trees but I don't like shrubs.

I like coffee but I don't like tea.

I like spoons but I don't like knives.

I like settees but I don't like sofas.

I like slippers but I don't like shoes.

Can you spot the link between the likes and dislikes? All the likes are words that have double letters in them, whereas the dislikes do not. You might choose something similar, or you might choose words with certain letters in them, or words that end in 'ing', or whatever you like. The only rule is that the 'like' word and the 'dislike' word have to have something in common. The first player to spot what it is the leader likes and dislikes becomes the leader in the next round.

Little and Large

Central Circles

Which of these two central circles is the larger?

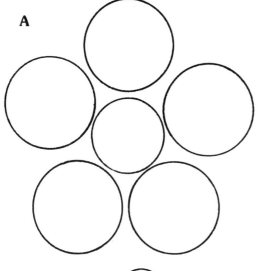

A

B

Longest Line

Which of these three lines is the longest?

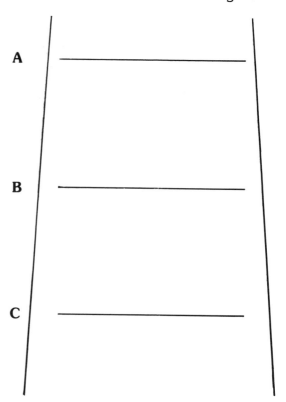

A

B

C

Longer Line

Which of these two lines is the longer?

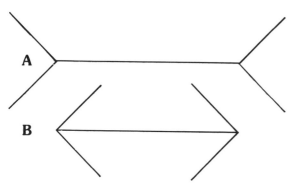

A

B

Matchstick Men

Which of these four men is the tallest?

A

B

C

D

Tallest Building

Which is the tallest of these three buildings?

1. The World Trade Centre, New York.
2. The Sears Tower, Chicago.
3. The Empire State Building, New York.

Largest Palace

Which is the largest of these three palaces?

1. Buckingham Palace.
2. Holyrood House.
3. Versailles.

Largest Block of Flats

Where are the largest blocks of private flats in Britain?

1. In the West End of London.
2. In the Barbican area of London.
3. In Birmingham.

Smallest House

Where is the smallest house in Britain?

1. In Cornwall.
2. In Wales.
3. In Scotland.

Largest Ship

Which is the largest passenger ship ever built?

1. The *Queen Elizabeth*.
2. The *Queen Elizabeth 2*.
3. The *Norway*.

Largest Bookshop

Which is the world's largest bookshop, in terms of the number of titles and length of shelving?

1. W. H. Smith in Bristol.
2. Foyles in London.
3. The Penguin Bookshop in New York.

Highest Mountain

Which is the highest mountain in the UK?

1. Scafell Pike.
2. Ben Nevis.
3. Mount Snowdon.

Shortest River

Which is the world's shortest river?

1. The River Bride in Dorset.
2. The River Severn in Canada.
3. The D River in Lincoln City, Oregon, USA.

Longest-reigning King

Which *king* of England reigned the longest?

1. Edward III.
2. Charles II.
3. George III.

Shortest-reigning Monarch

Which *king* or *queen* of England had the shortest reign?

1. Harold II.
2. Edward V.
3. Jane.

Largest City

Which is the largest city in the world in terms of population?

1. London.
2. Mexico City.
3. Tokyo.

Smallest Stamp

Who issued the smallest postage stamp in the world?

1. Guyana.
2. Norway.
3. The Colombian State of Bolivar.

Limericks

Most people know the kind of verse called the limerick, which was made famous by Edward Lear in the nineteenth century. Here is a typical Lear limerick:

> There was an old man of West Dumpet
> Who possessed a large nose like a trumpet;
> When he blew it aloud
> It astonished the crowd
> And was heard through the whole of West Dumpet.

The first, second and fifth lines rhyme; and the third and fourth lines rhyme. Lear often used the same word to end the first and fifth lines, but not always:

> There was an old man of the coast
> Who placidly sat on a post;
> But when it was cold
> He relinquished his hold
> And called for some hot buttered toast.

A group of people can have great fun playing a game with limericks. They sit round in a circle, and the first person makes up the first line, the second person the second line, the third the third line, and so on. You need to be fairly strict and only give each person half a minute to make up a line, or the game can go on for too long. The resulting limerick does not have to make *perfect* sense, but it does have to have the same rhyme and rhythm pattern of those quoted above.

Lipograms

What on earth is a lipogram, I hear you asking. Well, it is a version of a well-known poem or other piece of literature from which one or more letters of the alphabet have been deliberately excluded. For example, here is 'Mary Had a Little Lamb'.

> Mary had a little lamb,
> Its fleece was white as snow.
> And everywhere that Mary went
> The lamb was sure to go.
> It followed her to school one day,
> That was against the rule;
> It made the children laugh and play
> To see a lamb in school.

And here is the same verse rewritten, using no letter E. E is the most difficult letter to omit because it is the commonest in the English language.

> Mary had a tiny lamb,
> Its wool was pallid as snow.
> And any spot that Mary did walk
> This lamb was sure to go.
> This lamb did follow Mary to school,
> Although against the law;
> How girls and boys did laugh and play —
> That lamb in class all saw.

Have a go at some well-known nursery rhymes, omitting different letters. Its fun to do, and a useful exercise because it helps you to express the same idea in different ways.

Musical Medley

What's in a Name?

This pop group's name sounds as if it is connected with cars. What is it?

It's Instrumental

Find the thirty musical instruments listed below and hidden in this word-search puzzle. They may read across, down or diagonally, either forwards or backwards, but they are always in straight lines.

BANJO	**FRENCH HORN**	**PIANO**
BASSOON	**GLOCKENSPIEL**	**SITAR**
BUGLE	**GONG**	**TAMBOURINE**
CASTANETS	**GUITAR**	**TOM-TOM**
CONCERTINA	**HARP**	**TRIANGLE**
CYMBALS	**KETTLE DRUM**	**TROMBONE**
DOUBLE BASS	**LUTE**	**TUBA**
FIDDLE	**LYRE**	**VIOLIN**
FLUGELHORN	**MOUTH ORGAN**	**XYLOPHONE**
FLUTE	**OBOE**	**ZITHER**

```
F G L O C K E N S P I E L O N A I P
I L S E X O E B S S E L G N A I R T
D S U S N Y N T Z I T H E R G B P Q
D E T G A I L C T B T E S P R A N S
L R R U E B R O E L U A N Z O N O L
E Y O I G L E U P R E G R A H J O A
E L M T K N H L O H T D L B T O S B
T U B A Z A O O B B O I R E U S S M
U T O R R B N G R U M N N U O X A Y
L E N P V I O L I N O A E A M B B C
F R E N C H H O R N M D T O M T O M
```

108

Pop the Question

These records were all hits a year or two ago. Can you match them with the recording artistes listed? The hits include LPs and singles and not all the stars listed have a record here.

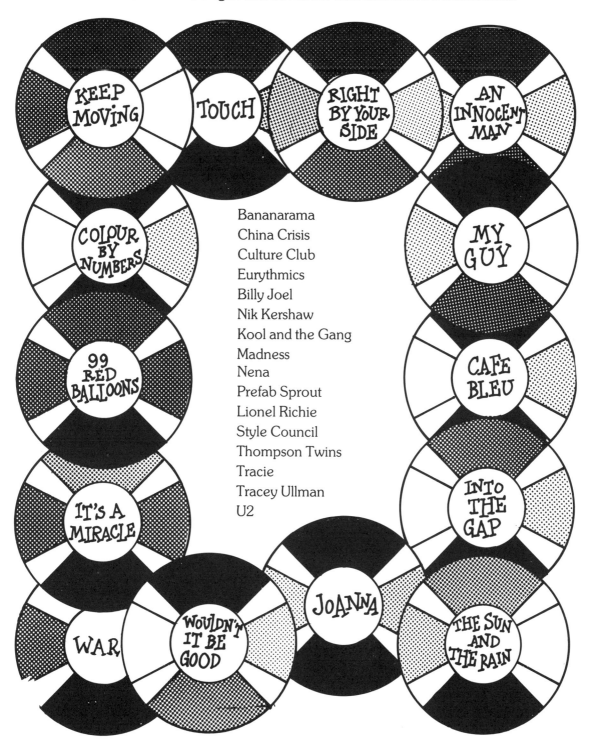

KEEP MOVING

TOUCH

RIGHT BY YOUR SIDE

AN INNOCENT MAN

COLOUR BY NUMBERS

MY GUY

99 RED BALLOONS

CAFE BLEU

IT'S A MIRACLE

INTO THE GAP

WAR

WOULDN'T IT BE GOOD

JOANNA

THE SUN AND THE RAIN

Bananarama
China Crisis
Culture Club
Eurythmics
Billy Joel
Nik Kershaw
Kool and the Gang
Madness
Nena
Prefab Sprout
Lionel Richie
Style Council
Thompson Twins
Tracie
Tracey Ullman
U2

Groovy!

How many grooves has a long-playing record on each side? The answer is not to be found in the maze, the object of which is to travel from the notch on the outside to the centre of the record.

Bits and Pieces

This unusual picture of a well-known pop singer has been cut up and the pieces stuck down in the wrong order. Do you recognize her?

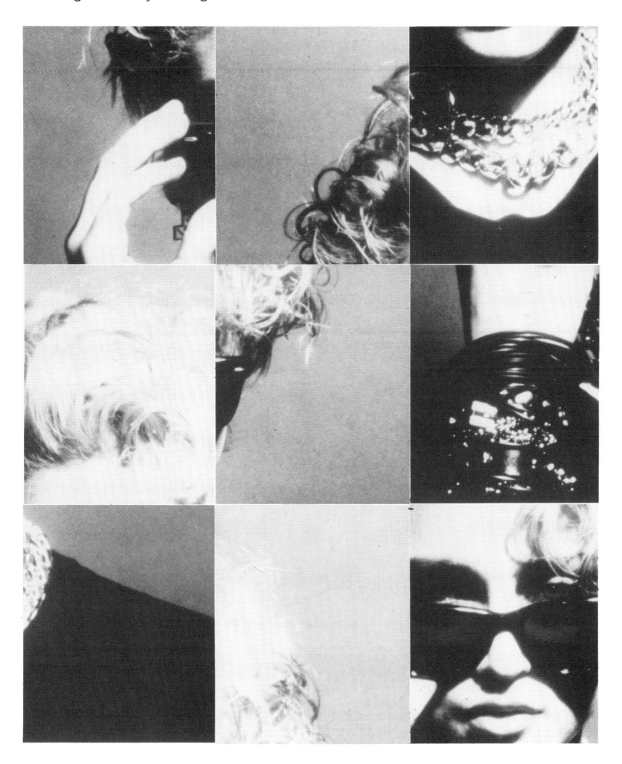

Pop Party

Fifty-two questions on pop old and new.

Places

1. Which city did Frank Sinatra call 'my kind of town'?
2. According to the Animals, where was the House of the Rising Sun?
3. To which American state did John Denver's 'country roads' take him?
4. Who went into 'Exile on Main Street'?
5. In which European country was Bonnie Tyler lost for her first hit?
6. Which American state did Ray Charles have on his mind?

Events

1. Whose hair caught fire while he was filming a Pepsi advert?
2. Who made a hit with the hymn 'All Things Bright and Beautiful'?
3. Who shocked a nation when they 'rocked round the clock'?
4. In which European city did John Lennon and Yoko Ono stage their first 'Bed In'?
5. Whose record 'Freight Train' started a skiffle boom?
6. Which male pop star came tenth on a 1973 list of the world's worst-dressed women?

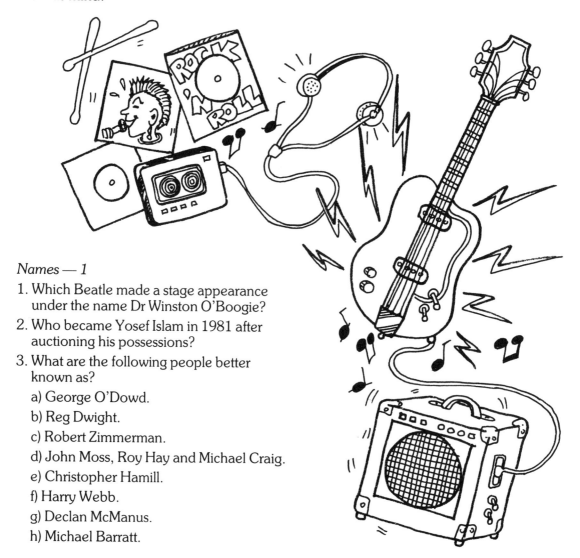

Names — 1

1. Which Beatle made a stage appearance under the name Dr Winston O'Boogie?
2. Who became Yosef Islam in 1981 after auctioning his possessions?
3. What are the following people better known as?

   a) George O'Dowd.

   b) Reg Dwight.

   c) Robert Zimmerman.

   d) John Moss, Roy Hay and Michael Craig.

   e) Christopher Hamill.

   f) Harry Webb.

   g) Declan McManus.

   h) Michael Barratt.

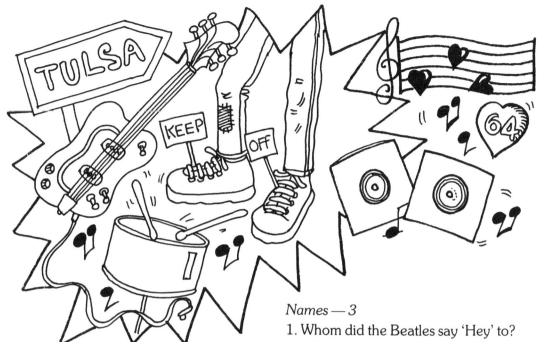

Names — 2

Who are these stars?

1. S H R E W J A D O N O.
2. P I E B A C T I N A N L E S S.
3. O S T Y M A I L O N E.
4. R T A P C L U N M A C E Y.
5. T R A I N R U N E T.
6. H E J O T N D L N.
7. T R A D O W E S T.
8. S N I D R O A S A.

Numbers and Colours

1. How many hours from Tulsa was Gene Pitney?
2. Who was 'A Little Red Rooster'?
3. According to Paul Simon, how many ways are there to leave your lover?
4. At what height did the Byrds fly?
5. Who said, 'You can do anything but don't step on my blue suede shoes'?
6. Who asked if they would still be loved when they were sixty-four?

Names — 3

1. Whom did the Beatles say 'Hey' to?
2. Who was Neil Diamond's 'cracklin'' girl?
3. Whom did the Beach Boys meet when they went to a dance, looking for romance?
4. Which of Marilyn Monroe's husbands is named in 'Mrs Robinson'?
5. Whose LP was named after the American outlaw John Wesley Hardin?
6. Which girl's name did Chuck Berry rhyme with the title of the rock and roll classic 'Memphis, Tennessee'?

Mistakes

Each of these pop titles has one word wrong. Can you put it right?

1. 'Mill of Kintyre'.
2. 'Lie Just a Little Bit'.
3. 'Bat Rapping'.
4. 'Lost for Life'.
5. 'Jumping Back Flash'.
6. 'Christmas Chameleon'.
7. 'Ain't No Ladder High Enough'.
8. 'Crimson Submarine'.
9. 'Everything I Owe'.
10. 'I Wanna Kiss Your Hand'.

Musical Games

For all these games you will, of course, need a source of music, but for some of them this could be the players' voices.

Musical Chairs

You need six or more players, and one chair fewer than the number of players to play Musical Chairs.

The chairs are placed in the centre of the room with the seats facing outwards, and the players form a ring round the chairs, holding hands. Someone needs to be on hand to start the music, and when they do, the players start to dance round the chairs. As soon as the music stops, the players rush to the nearest chair and sit down on it. As there are fewer chairs than players, one person will be left without a chair, and that person is out of the game and should leave the circle, taking one chair with them. The game continues in this way until one player manages to grab the last chair and thus wins the game.

The Grand Old Duke of York

This is a game for an even number of players, and needs eight or more for it to be successful. Ideally, the song 'The Grand Old Duke of York' should be played on a record player and the players sing along with it, but if you don't have a record of it the players can just sing it, as most people will know the tune. The words of the song are given below.

Players take partners and line up facing each other in two equal rows. They start to sing the song, and the players at the top of the line hold hands and skip together down the middle of the rows of players and back again, singing as they go. As they reach their places again at the top of the row, they let go of their hands and march back to the bottom of the line behind the other players. When they reach the bottom of the line they take their places again there and continue singing, while the pair who are now at the top of the line join hands and skip down the middle as before. The game continues until every couple has had a turn at dancing down the middle and back again and finally takes their places at the bottom of the line.

Here are the words of the song, in case you are not sure of them.

> O the Grand Old Duke of York,
> He had ten thousand men,
> He marched them up to the top of the hill,
> And he marched them down again.
> And when they were up, they were up,
> And when they were down, they were
>   down,
> And when they were only half way up
> They were neither up nor down!

Here We Go Round the Mulberry Bush

This is a game for any number of fairly young children to play. Again, if you have the music to play, so much the better, but otherwise the players' singing will suffice. It is helpful to have an adult or an older child to lead the others in the singing and the game.

The players join hands and dance round in a circle singing:

> Here we go round the mulberry bush,
> The mulberry bush, the mulberry bush,
> Here we go round the mulberry bush,
> On a cold and frosty morning.

Then they stop dancing, and sing the next verse, meanwhile miming the actions as they do so.

> This is the way we clap our hands,
> Clap our hands, clap our hands,
> This is the way we clap our hands,
> On a cold and frosty morning.

Then they form a circle again, and dance round singing the first verse again. This is followed by standing still and singing and performing the second mime, which can be anything from 'brush our hair' to 'scrub the floor', and which follows the pattern of the second verse. The game continues in this way, with dancing and singing the first verse followed by standing still and miming the next, and the actions can be anything that is reasonably simple to mime. The game can thus continue for as long as the players' energy and the leader's imagination allow.

Musical Posture

This is a game for any number of players, and requires a book for each participant. It needs someone to start and stop the music.

This game may improve the players' posture, but it will certainly cause a lot of amusement. Each player balances their book carefully on their head and walks round the room while the music is playing. When the music stops the player must stop, go down on one knee, raise both hands in the air and stand up again, without dropping the book. Any player who does drop a book is out of the game. When all the players have done the action the music starts again and the players walk round as before. The game continues until there is only one player left in the game, and he or she is the winner.

Paul Jones

Any number of people can play this game, though it is best to have quite a lot of players. Someone is needed to stop and start the music, and set the tasks which are performed.

The players form two circles, the girls forming an inner circle facing outwards, and the boys forming an outer circle facing

inwards. When the music starts, the two circles of players start to dance round, one circle going in the opposite direction to the other. When the music stops, a boy should be facing a girl, and they are told to perform certain tasks. For example, one might be asked to dance round the other, or both might be asked to hop round on one leg, or shake hands left-handedly. The tasks should not be too complicated, or such that they will cause embarrassment for shy players. After the task is completed, the music is started again.

The music should be stopped, if possible, when different players are facing each other, so that by the end of the game each player in the inner circle will have had an opportunity of meeting each player in the outer circle.

Musical Statues

Four or more players are needed for this game, and again someone is needed to control the music, and to judge the players.

The music played should be good and lively, and the players all dance energetically round the room. When the music stops, whatever they are doing, they must 'freeze' in that position and not move a muscle. If they giggle, or wobble, or fall over, then they are out of the game. The music should be played for quite a long time in the first place, to lull the players into a false sense of security, but it should not be stopped for too long, or all the players will be out. Gradually, however, the music can be played for shorter periods, and the stopping periods can be lengthened a little, to make it more difficult. The last person left in the game is the winner.

Making Music

You can make your very own musical instrument if you have eight small glass bowls or glasses. You have to fill each bowl or glass to a different level with water, and then you can produce a different note on each. A small amount of water gives a high note, a greater amount gives a low note, and the glasses are played by means of a moistened finger run round the rim of the glass, which should also be moistened.

If you fill the glasses as shown below, they should produce the notes indicated. You may need to experiment a little until you get it right. To make it easier to tell the glasses apart, you could colour the water in them differently using food colourings.

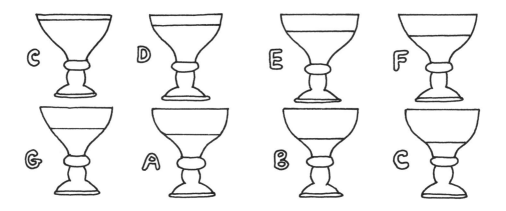

When you try to play the glasses, as described above, both your finger and the glass's rim should be moistened. When you run your finger round the rim of the glass it should produce a clear, ringing sound. If you have difficulty in producing this sound, try reversing the direction in which you are running your finger round the glass, and the sound should be produced easily. You can use a tuning-fork to check the notes produced, but if you have a reasonably good ear you will be able to manage without.

When you have made your musical instrument, you can teach yourself to play tunes on it.

Musical Miscellany

Musicals

1. Which musical was based on Shakespeare's play *Romeo and Juliet*?
2. Which musical was based on Shakespeare's play *The Taming of the Shrew*?
3. On whose poems was the musical *Cats* based?

4. Which musical was based on stories about pre-war Berlin?
5. Which musical was named after the wife of a South American dictator?

A Night at the Opera

1. What is unusual about the opera *Billy Budd*?
2. By which name is the operetta *The Town of Titipu* better known?
3. Which opera is about a legendary sailor cursed to roam the seas forever?
4. In which opera does the villain Scarpia appear?
5. *The Marriage of Figaro* and *The Barber of Seville* are both about the same character. Were the operas written by the same person?
6. Which opera is about a gypsy girl who worked in a cigarette factory?
7. The opera *Aida* was written to commemorate the opening of the Suez Canal. True or false?
8. Which opera is based on Dumas's *The Lady of the Camellias*?

People and Instruments

1. For what are a) Andrew and b) Julian Lloyd Webber famous?
2. Which of these composers are known for their piano music: Chopin, Liszt, Mahler?
3. Which is the odd man out: clarinet, trombone, trumpet?
4. How many strings has a guitar?
5. With which instruments are the following people associated:
   a) Julian Bream?
   b) Pablo Casals?
   c) James Galway?
   d) Yehudi Menuhin?
6. Who wrote 'The Four Seasons'?
7. Which Finnish composer wrote music relating to Finland's epic poems?
8. Who wrote the Brandenburg Concertos?
9. How do you play a euphonium?
10. Which instrument has a higher pitch, the violin or the viola?
11. Which of the following are percussion instruments: tambourine, cornet, marimba, glockenspiel, tuba?

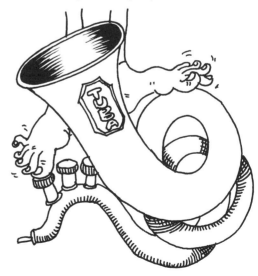

12. Who wrote 'The Carnival of the Animals'?

Nursery Rhymes

Beginnings...

The following are the first lines of twenty well-known nursery rhymes — though something has happened to make them difficult to recognize. Can you identify them all?

1. R A T S E L T T I L E L K N I W T E L K N I W T
2. J C K N D J L L W N T P T H H L L
3. L D M T H R H B B R D W N T T T H C P B R D
4. S N E T T I M R I E H T T S O L Y E H T S N E T T I K E L T T I L E E R H T
5. T E F F U T A N O T A S T E F F U M S S I M E L T T I L
6. M R Y M R Y Q T C N T R R Y
7. G R G P R G P D D N G N D P
8. L T T L B Y B L C M B L W Y R H R N
9. N H O J N O S Y M G N I L P M U D E L D D I D E L D D I D
10. P S S Y C T P S S Y C T W H R H V Y B N
11. S S O R C Y R U B N A B O T E S R O H K C O C A E D I R
12. R I A F E H T O T G N I O G N A M E I P A T E M N O M I S E L P M I S
13. T H R W S L T T L G R L W H H D L T T L C R L
14. T H Q N F H R T S S H M D S M T R T S
15. E C N E P X I S F O G N O S A G N I S
16. L O O W Y N A U O Y E V A H P E E H S K C A L B A A B A A B
17. L T T L B P P S H L S T H R S H P
18. H C K R Y D C K R Y D C K
19. W W L L W N K R N S T H R G H T H T W N
20. R E D N A G Y E S O O G Y E S O O G

118

... and Endings

These are the last lines of ten equally well-known rhymes. Can you identify them?

1. And the dish ran away with the spoon.
2. So early in the morning.
3. And whipped them all soundly, and sent them to bed.
4. Turn 'em out, knaves all three!
5. And put it in the oven for baby and me.
6. Because I am good.
7. For if I do, he's sure to cry.
8. And pretty maids all in a row.
9. With vinegar and brown paper.
10. She shall have music wherever she goes.

Who?

More nursery-rhyme questions.

1. Wandered in my lady's chamber?
2. Rapped at the window and cried through the lock?
3. Left their tails behind them?
4. Was in the parlour, eating bread and honey?
5. Sat among the cinders and got whipped?
6. Could eat no fat?
7. Rides hobbledy-hoy, hobbledy-hoy?
8. Had not a penny?
9. Bought her dog some fish?
10. Ate curds and whey?

Needle in a Haystack

There is just one NEEDLE hidden in this haystack. It may be written across, down or diagonally, either forwards or backwards, but it is in a straight line. Can you find it?

```
L D E N E E D E L N E E N E D
E E N E D L E N E E D E L N E
E E L E N D L E E D E N E E D
D N E L E E N E L E E L E E N
E E L D E E D N L E D E N D E
N L E E D E L E D E E N E L E
E D E N N E E L E D L E N D E
E D E L E E D N E E L D E L L
L E N E L D L E N E E L D N E
D E D L N E E D L E N E E D
E L D E L N E L E N E D E D N
E E D N E D E D E E D E N L E
E L D E E E E L N E E L E D E
E D E L D E N E E D L N E E L
N D E E L E N E N E E L D E E
```

120

Numbing Number Puzzles

The Missing Numbers

Many sayings, and the titles of books, films and plays have numbers in them. Can you fill in the missing numbers in the examples below? Titles of books, films and plays are printed in italics.

1. A stitch in time saves ——————.
2. The Famous ——————.
3. The Secret ——————.
4. —————— *Leagues Under The Sea.*
5. —————— *Men in a Boat.*
6. *The* —————— *Musketeers.*
7. *The* —————— *Steps.*
8. *The* —————— *Years' War.*
9. At —————— and ——————.
10. A bird in the hand is worth —————— in the bush.

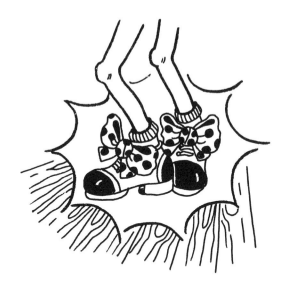

Complete the Box

What is the number missing from the box?

9	39	27
3	15	15
6	24	

Eight Eights

Using an 8,
  and an 8,
    and an 8,
      and an 8,
        and an 8,
          and an 8,
            and an 8,
              and one more 8
can you make a simple sum that adds up to 1000?

Treading the Boards

The Tweazleton Twinkletoes dancing group has quite a lot of members. If they perform a routine in threes, one of them is left out. If they perform in fours, two are left out; if they perform in fives, three are left out; and if they perform in sixes, four are left out. How many members does the group have?

Spending Power

After Brenda Biggins had paid a visit to Mrs Tilly's Tuck Shop, she had 60p in her purse. In Mrs Tilly's she had spent a third and a quarter of the money she had originally. How much money was there in her purse when she entered the shop?

Three Dozen

Three dozen, 3 x 12, is 36. Another way of looking at 36 is to say that it is made up of four numbers, which can be treated in the following way and the results still add up to 36. You can add 2 to one of the numbers, subtract 2 from one of the numbers, multiply one of the numbers by 2 and divide one of the numbers by 2, and the results you are left with will still add up to 36. How do you divide 36 to be able to do this?

Odd Man Out

Can you spot the odd man out in these collections of numbers?

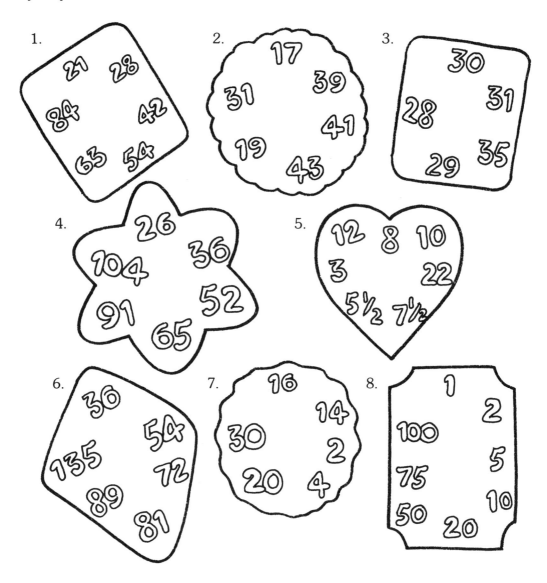

1. 21 28 84 42 63 54
2. 17 31 39 19 41 43
3. 30 28 31 29 35
4. 26 104 36 91 52 65
5. 12 8 10 3 22 5½ 7½
6. 36 54 135 72 89 81
7. 16 14 30 2 20 4
8. 1 2 100 5 75 50 10 20

Next, Please

What is the next number in the series?

7 13 9 16 13 20 21 25 37 —

Trick Question

There is a trick involved here, but the puzzle is possible to solve. Here it is: from 19 take one away and leave 20.

Score a Century

Can you arrange these digits in a simple sum that will add up to 100?

Magic Number Squares

Do you know what a magic number square is? It is one in which every line, column or diagonal adds up to the same number. If you look at the square below, you will see that each line, column or diagonal adds up 65.

17	24	1	8	15
23	5	7	14	16
4	6	13	20	22
10	12	19	21	3
11	18	25	2	9

If you increase every number by the same amount, you can create a new magic square. In the example below, 5 has been added to each number.

22	29	6	13	20
28	10	12	19	21
9	11	18	25	27
15	17	24	26	8
16	23	30	7	14

Each line, column and diagonal now adds up to 90.

Using the above square as a guide, fill in the gaps in the square below.

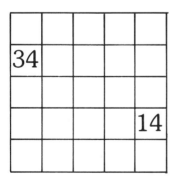

Symbolic

In this square, each symbol stands for a different number. The numbers, when added together, again total the amounts at the ends of the lines and columns, and are all between 1 and 6.

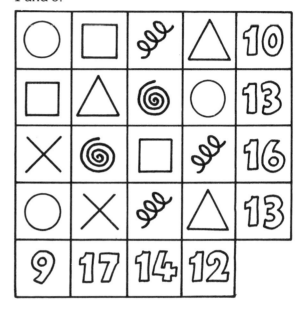

Figure It Out

Take the numbers from 1 to 10 and divide them into five pairs of figures in such a way that one pair adds up to 6, one pair adds up to 7, one pair adds up to 9, one pair adds up to 16 and one pair adds up to 17.

Odd Number

While we're on the subject of numbers, get a piece of paper and a pencil and try writing this one down: eleven thousand, eleven hundred and eleven. Can you do it?

Round Dozen

Using one plus sign and a fraction, can you make six ones add up to twelve?

Digital Daze

Find a four-digit number in which the last digit is twice the first, the second digit is three less than the third, and if you add the first digit to the last digit the answer is twice the third digit.

Two Twos

In this figure you should be able to find the word 'two' written out twice. The words may be written across, down or diagonally, either forwards or backwards, but they are in straight lines.

```
O W O T O T O T O T
T T O O W O W O O W O O
W O W O T O W O T O T T W
W O O T                 T O W O
                        W O T W
                        W W O O
                        T W T W
                      W O W W O
                    T O O O W
                  T O T W W
                T O W O W
              T T T O W
            O W O T T
          T W T W T
        W T O T O
      W O W W W
      W O T O T T O W O W O W W
      T O W O W O O T T W T W T
      W O T W W O O O W O W O O
```

Three Threes

In this figure you should be able to find the word 'three' written out three times. Again, the words may be read across, down or diagonally, either forwards or backwards, but they are in straight lines.

```
        T R E E T H
       T H R R E E R T
      R H E E T H R T R E
     H T E E H E R T H E E R
    T H E R T H E E R T H E
                    E R T E
                    T R E E
           R E H T E R E H T
         T R E E E H R E H T
         T H R T E R H E R
         E T H E R E E H T T
          T H T E E R E T H
                    T E E T
                    H R E E
      T E E T H R E H T H R E
      R T E T H R E T R T T H
      R H E T T R E E T H
        T H E R T E T E
         T E T H R E
```

Opposites

Match the words in the first balloon with their opposites in the second balloon.

body war famous
sour near
silence straight
prologue jagged private
safe reactionary
flexible nadir
noxious monotony
happiness broken novel
vanish

epilogue traditional
variety sweet
unknown peace rigid
misery wholesome
curved whole
progressive zenith smooth
hazardous materialize
public mind noise
far

Outsiders

Spot the outsiders in each of these groups of objects.

Observation Test

Market Stalls

Study this busy market day scene for one minute (time yourself with a watch), then cover the picture with a sheet of paper, turn the book upside down, and see how many of the questions you can answer about the picture.

10. Who has a balloon?
9. How many people are wearing spectacles?
8. What is the lady with the hat buying?
7. What is the policeman doing with his hands?
6. What is on a stick under the awning?

5. Who has a moustache and a spotted tie?
4. What time is it by the church clock?
3. How many children are there in the picture?
2. How much are pillows?
1. How much are pears?

128

Building Site

You are unlikely ever to see a building site like this one! The artist has made fifteen deliberate mistakes in the picture. How many can you spot?

Oranges and Lemons

This popular game is best played with eight or more players. Two grown-ups, or the two tallest children, form an arch with their hands held high above their heads. One of them is to be head of the oranges team, and one to be head of the lemons team, positions which are decided before the game starts.

The other players form a chain, each holding onto the waist of the player in front. They go under the arch, singing the oranges and lemons song, and as the final word 'head' is sung, the players forming the arch drop their hands and catch the player passing underneath. He or she is asked in a whisper which of the two sides of the arch — the orange or the lemon — he or she wishes to join. Whichever side the player chooses, he or she stands behind the leader and holds on to their waist. Eventually as the game progresses the orange and lemon leaders build up equal-sized teams, which, when the last player has been caught, have a tug of war.

Here are the words of the 'Oranges and Lemons' song.

'Oranges and lemons,'
Say the bells of St Clement's.
'Bulls'-eyes and targets,'
Say the bells of St Margaret's.
'Brickbats and tiles,'
Say the bells of St Giles'.
'Pancakes and fritters,'
Say the bells of St Peter's.
'Two sticks and an apple,'
Say the bells of Whitechapel.
'Old Father Baldpate,'
Say the slow bells of Aldgate.
'Maids in white aprons,'
Say the bells of St Catherine's.
'Pokers and tongs,'
Say the bells of St John's.
'Kettles and pans,'
Say the bells of St Anne's.
'You owe me five farthings,'
Say the bells of St Martin's.
'When will you pay me?'
Say the bells of Old Bailey.
'When I grow rich,'
Say the bells of Shoreditch.
'Pray when will that be?'
Say the bells of Stepney.
* 'I'm sure I don't know,'
* Says the great bell of Bow.
Here comes a candle to light you to bed.
Here comes a chopper to chop off your head!

The 'St Clement's', 'St Margaret's' and so on in the song are London churches.

* *These lines should be sung slowly and solemnly.*

Owl and Ostrich

All the twenty-five words in this word-search puzzle either begin with or end in O. The words may be read across, down or diagonally, either forwards or backwards, but always in straight lines.

CELLO	OASIS	OLIVE	OSTRICH	OWL
ESKIMO	OCTAVE	ONCE	OTHER	POLO
IGLOO	OFFICE	OPEN	OUT	SOLO
LOTTO	OIL	OPERA	OVAL	TABOO
OAR	OLD	ORANGE	OVER	TACO

```
        O O O O
      O O U O F O L O
    O O T O O O F V I O
  O O R O O L L A I O O O
  S O L A I D L O R C L O
O I O L G N O E H A E E W O
O S Q L O O G C T O O P O O
O A O O E P I E S K I M O O
O O O C O R O O L O O O A O
O N O T A B O O O O R R
O O S L A O O T H E R O
  O P O I V O T V O O
    O E O V E O O O
        N O E O
```

Ornithological

Do you know what 'ornithological' means? It means 'connected with birds', and this is what this crossword is. All the answers are kinds of birds.

Across
2. A small bird which is very active and acrobatic (6).
5. The redbreasted bird shown on Christmas cards (5).
7. A large bird of prey with keen eyesight (5).
8. A slender, heron-like wading bird (5).
9. A bird associated with New Zealand (4).
10. A bird which is the name of a chesspiece (4).

Down
1. A small songbird of the finch family (6).
2. A farmyard bird eaten at Christmas (6).
3. A long-tailed black and white bird of the crow family (6).
4. Another name for the lapwing (6).
6. A night-time bird, considered to be wise (4, 3).

Party Time

Party Food

Can you work out from these muddled labels what the sandwich fillings are? And when you've done that, can you say how many of each kind of sandwich are on each plate?

Party People

When the Browns and the Smiths got together for a party, all the Browns wore party hats, and all the Smiths had balloons. How many of each family are shown in the picture?

Party Games

Let your hair down with these traditional party games.

Sardines

This is an amusing game for six or more players. Ideally it should be played in a large house which has lots of places in which to hide.

The game starts with all the players assembling in one room. One player then leaves that room and goes to hide somewhere in the house. After a minute has passed, another player leaves, with the object of finding the first player and joining him or her in the hiding-place. The other players follow at one-minute intervals, each one who finds the others joining them in the hiding-place until all the players are squashed together, like sardines in a can. The game has no winner, and no losers, unless someone cannot find the others, but it is always a lot of fun to play.

Apple Ducking

Unless you have a large waterproof sheet, or lots of newspapers, this game is best played out of doors. You will need a bowl of water and as many apples as there are players. Any number of people can play.

Fill the bowl to just below its surface with water. If you have more than six players you may need two bowls of water. Float the apples on the water. The object then is for each player, kneeling by the bowl and with their hands behind their backs, to try and lift an apple from the bowl using only their mouths and teeth. The first person to do so is the winner.

Hunt the Thimble

This is a game for four or more players, and requires a thimble or other small object.

One player is chosen to 'hide' the thimble while the others are out of the room. He or she should not really hide it, but place it where it can be seen but not easily spotted, such as among the ornaments on a mantelpiece, in a potted plant, and so on.

The other players then re-enter the room and begin to hunt the thimble. When someone spots it he or she sits down without saying anything and without drawing attention to the thimble's location. The last player to spot the thimble and sit down is the loser, and it is his or her task to 'hide' the thimble on the next round.

The Donkey's Tail

This game can be played by any number of people, but before you start you need a large drawing of a donkey, a separate tail, a notice board or blackboard to which they can be pinned, a blindfold, a drawing pin, and some chalk or marker pens or pins. The reasons for all these things will become apparent shortly.

The idea is to have a large drawing or paper cut-out donkey stuck onto the blackboard or notice board, and to give each player, who must be blindfolded, a chance to pin his tail into the right position. The tail can either be made of paper, or can simply be a length of string, but one end of it should have a drawing-pin in it to enable it to be pinned in place. Care should be taken when handing the tail to the blindfolded player so they don't get the drawing-pin stuck in their fingers.

No matter how carefully the players study the donkey before they start, their attempts to pin on the tail are usually hilarious! Before the tail is removed to let the next player have a go,

its position should be marked, either with a chalk mark and the player's name drawn on the blackboard, or with little labels and marker pins stuck in the notice board, or with marker pens if the donkey is surrounded by a large sheet of white paper.

When all the players have had a turn, the player whose attempt came nearest to the correct position of the donkey's tail wins.

Newspaper Fancy Dress

Any number of people can play this game. You will need for each player a newspaper and some sticky tape.

It is a game for those with imagination and a bit of handicraft skill, for each player is given one large newspaper and a roll of sticky tape (or two players can share a roll if there isn't enough to go round), and allowed ten minutes to fashion a fancy-dress costume.

When the ten minutes are up the players parade round the room, and the winner is the person who, in the opinion of the majority, has created the cleverest, most amusing or most original costume. If the costumes hold together, the players may like to keep them on for the rest of the party.

The Judge

Any even number of players can play this game, plus one extra person to be the Judge.

With the exception of the Judge, the players form pairs and sit on the floor. The Judge remains standing, and when the game begins, marches up and down the room. Suddenly he turns to one partner of a pair of players and asks him or her a question. However, it is the *other* partner of the pair who has to answer him. If the player questioned answers, or if his or her partner fails to answer, then that pair is out of the game.

The game can be made very exciting if the Judge cleverly makes up questions that he knows the person to whom they are directed will be longing to answer, while the partner will be reluctant to do so.

Play continues until only one pair is left in the game, and they become the winners.

Act the Word

This game can be played by any number of players. One player leaves the room while the others choose a word, which must be an adverb, or word that describes how an action is performed, such as 'quickly', 'slowly', 'carefully', 'energetically', etc.

The player who left the room then re-enters, and it is his or her job to guess the chosen word. In order to do this he or she asks one of the other players to perform a task, such as 'read a book', 'polish a table', 'drive a car' in the manner of the word. If the player cannot guess the word from the other player's action, then he or she can ask a second player to demonstrate it, and if still stuck, players can drop useful hints. But it is better to choose a simple word that can be guessed quickly, and keep the game moving. Once the word has been guessed, another player leaves the room and a second word is chosen by those who remain.

Sausages

Sausages is a very silly game that any number of people can play. All you need is for one person to be chosen as the victim (players should take it in turns), while all the other players fire random questions at him or her.

To each question, no matter what it is, the victim has to answer 'sausages'. And while doing so, no matter how much all the other players are rolling about with laughter, he or she has to keep a straight face. If they don't, then they are out of the game and someone else is chosen as victim.

This is how it works.

Anne: What's your favourite colour?

Victim: Sausages.

Mary: What sports do you enjoy playing?

Victim: Sausages.

Jim: What do you wear on your feet?

Victim: Sausages.

You can see how silly it gets!

Kim's Game

This is a good children's party game, but it can be played by any number of children and/or adults. It requires someone to prepare beforehand a tray or table covered with miscellaneous objects, and each player needs a pencil and a piece of paper.

On the tray or table should be placed twenty or thirty objects, ranging from the commonplace to the unusual. They might include, for example, a pencil sharpener, a hair grip, a teaspoon, a piece of string, a postage stamp, a photograph of a famous person or building, a clothes peg, a wrapped sweet, a tea bag, and so on. The objects are covered with a cloth until all the players are assembled, and then the cloth is removed and the players have thirty seconds in which to study the objects. The tray is then covered again, and the players have between three and five minutes in which to write down as many of the objects as possible. A point is scored for each object remembered correctly, but a point is deducted for any object listed that was not actually there. The player with the greatest number of points wins the game.

The Picture Frame Game

This is an amusing and silly game which demands great self control. It can be played by any number of people, and all that is required is an empty picture frame, or, failing that, a frame made out of cardboard.

Players take it in turns to hold up the picture frame for sixty seconds and to look through it at the others. The player looking through the frame has to keep an absolutely straight face, and neither speak, smile nor laugh, while the other players do their utmost to break his or her control by telling jokes, pulling faces and calling out silly remarks. The winner is the player who manages to keep a straight face for sixty seconds (or for as long as possible), and because the task is so difficult, he or she should be suitably rewarded.

Party Drinks

1. What fruit is cider made from?
2. What fruit is perry made from?
3. Coca Cola first appeared in the USA in 1885. True or false?
4. Who, according to history, drowned in a butt of malmsey?
5. What kind of drink is Earl Grey?
6. Where do people drink koumiss?
7. The world record for drinking two pints of milk is 3·2 seconds. True or false?
8. What is Perrier?
9. What is claret?
10. Which country does Guinness come from?

Parlez-vous?

Do you know what the following French words and phrases mean?

1. Parlez-vous français?
2. Café au lait.
3. A droit.
4. A gauche.
5. Dimanche.
6. Voilà.
7. Il est trois heures.
8. Vive la France!

Painters

What nationality were the following painters?

1. Leonardo da Vinci.
2. Picasso.
3. Van Gogh.
4. Monet.
5. Turner.
6. Rembrandt.

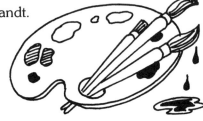

Picture Words

Can you work out the words and phrases depicted here?

1.  PROMISE

2. 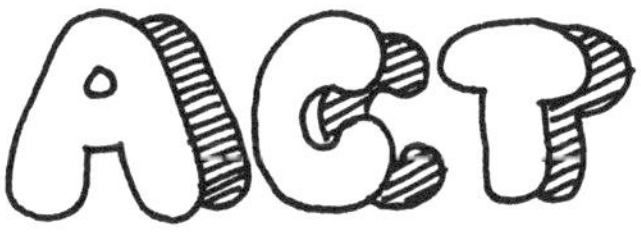 ACT

3. 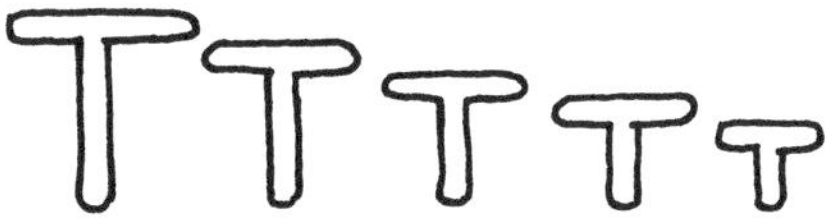 T T T T_T

4.

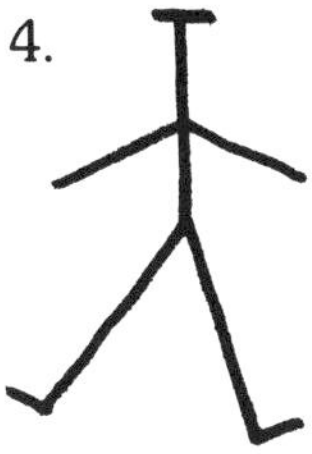

5.

6.  ADVi

7.  ME AL

8.  M M M M

9.  Shame

10.  (LL M N M N N)

11.  A S E (scattered letters)

12.

139

Paper Fun

Paper Puzzler

Take a piece of paper, a pencil, a pair of scissors, and some adhesive or adhesive tape.

Cut from the paper a strip about 5 cm (2 in) wide and about 60 cm (2 ft) long. Give the paper one twist, and then stick or tape the two ends together.

Now run your pencil all the way along the centre of the strip of paper. If you do this without lifting the pencil from the paper, you will discover that the end of your line meets its beginning, i.e. you will have made one continuous line, which proves that the paper has only one side!

Now try cutting along your pencil line to make your paper loop into two paper loops. What happens? It can't be done! You simply make one larger, continuous loop instead of two!

And if you then take the larger loop, and cut round it a third of the width from the edge all the way round, you will eventually produce two interlocking loops, one large one and one smaller one.

This extraordinary phenomenon was invented by a German mathematician who lived in the last century, called Ferdinand Mobius, and the strip of paper formed in this way is called a Mobius strip.

Strip Tease

Cut out four strips of paper, each about 50 cm (2 in) long. Two of the strips should be twice as wide as the other two.

Line them up like this and they all look the same length.

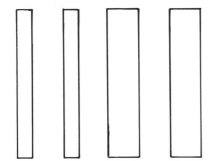

Now make a Z shape with the thicker strips at top and bottom. The narrow strip appears to have shrunk! Reverse the positions, i.e. put the narrow strips at the top and bottom of the Z, and they look longer than the thicker strip.

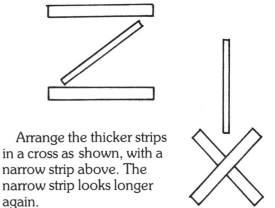

Arrange the thicker strips in a cross as shown, with a narrow strip above. The narrow strip looks longer again.

Make a cross from the narrow strips and place a thicker strip above, and now that looks longer. It's all very strange!

Blindfold Drawing

Any number of people can play this game. Each one needs a sheet of paper, a pencil, and a scarf or handkerchief to act as a blindfold. The game requires someone to act as instructor.

All the players sit at a table with their paper and pencil in front of them, and put on their blindfolds. The instructor then tells them to draw a picture of a house. When they have done this, they are told to draw a tree on the left of the house. Then they are asked to draw a garden in front of the house, with flowers in it. Then they are asked to draw some hills behind the house, and clouds in the sky. Finally, they are asked to draw a person in the garden, picking the flowers.

When all the drawings have been completed, the players remove their blindfolds and look at their own and other people's drawings. This is the time when everyone has a jolly good laugh, for most of the pictures will be complete nonsense!

Pencil and Paper Games

The games in this section are for two players.

Battleships

This game is said to have developed from games played by British prisoners of war in the First World War. But even if you don't like the idea of war games, it is amusing and exciting to play.

Before the game starts each player will need to draw up two identical grids ten squares across by ten squares down. Along the top the grids are lettered A to J, and down the left-hand side they are numbered 1 to 10. Thus any square can be immediately identified. One grid is headed HOME FLEET; the other ENEMY FLEET.

The players toss a coin to see who shall start. Each player has an imaginary fleet which he or she has to position in the HOME FLEET grid, taking care that the other player does not see it. Each player's fleet consists of:

one battleship (four squares long)

two cruisers (each three squares long)

three destroyers (each two squares long)

four submarines (each one square long)

The ships are positioned by outlining the appropriate number of squares in vertical or horizontal rows. At least one blank square must be left between ships.

The winner of the toss opens play by firing three shots, i.e. calling out three squares. He makes a note of which squares he has called by marking his ENEMY FLEET sheet. The opponent has to own up and say whether any of his or her ships has been hit, i.e. if any of the squares called were occupied by any of the opponent's ships, and what kind of ships they were. The player who fired the shots makes a note of this, too, on the ENEMY FLEET grid. A ship can only be sunk when all its squares have been called, but they don't all have to be called in one go, it can be progressively weakened by each shot.

It is then the turn of the other player, who follows exactly the same procedure. The aim of each player is to destroy the enemy fleet before their own is sunk, and the first one to do this wins the game.

Sample sheets for the game might look like this.

Home fleet

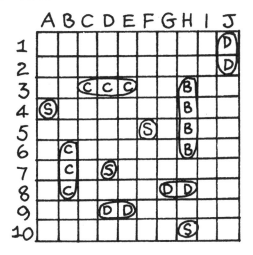

Enemy fleet

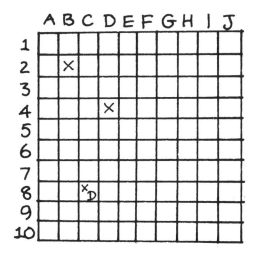

Join the Numbers

This is a simple game of skill that can be played almost anywhere. It requires one largish sheet of paper and two pencils.

The first player writes the numbers from 1 to 21 (in figures) higgledy piggledy on the paper, which he or she then passes to the other player, who does the same. The players then toss a coin to see who shall start, and the winner has to join two of the same numbers with a line. For example, they may join the two 5s, or the two 12s. The other player then joins two numbers with a line, and the play continues in this way, with each player taking a turn. However, no player may cross an existing line with a new line. The game continues until one player becomes completely stuck and unable to join any pair of numbers without crossing a line, and when this happens the other player becomes the winner.

Nine Holes

Nine holes is a very old game. It requires a grid like that below drawn on a piece of paper or card, and three counters — which may be 1p, 2p and 5p coins, or buttons of different colours.

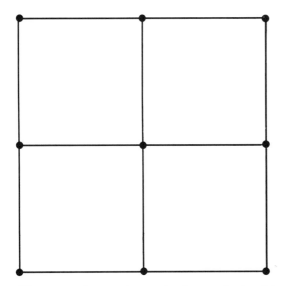

The game begins by each player placing his or her counters on the 'board' one at a time in turn. Each counter is placed on one of the

points where the lines intersect, and because the counters are placed on the board in turn, each player ensures that the other does not manage to place all three in a straight line, as this is the ultimate object of the game.

When all the counters are on the board, the players take turns to move one counter to an adjacent, unoccupied point, moving along one of the lines. The winner is the first person to get all the counters in a row.

The Worm

Before play can start in this game it requires ten rows of ten dots to be marked on a piece of paper.

The players toss a coin to see who shall start, and the winner of the toss draws a line either across or down to join two dots which are next to each other. Diagonal lines are not allowed. The second player draws another line, linking one end of the first line with another adjacent dot. Thus play proceeds, with players taking it in turns to create the 'worm'. The aim of each player is to force the other into a position where he or she can only draw a line which will join up with the main body of the 'worm', because that player will then be the loser.

In the example shown in the drawing, the next player will lose, for the only line that can be drawn will join up with the rest of the 'worm'.

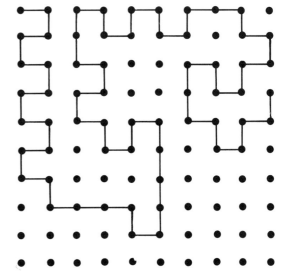

Picture Puzzles

These two sheepdogs have to take the sheep from the pen and add one to each of the six flocks, in order that each flock continues to spell out a word. Which sheep goes to which flock?

Getting the Bird

Each of these birds is made up from the letters of its name. What are the names?

144

P-p-p-perplexing

How many things beginning with P can you find in this picture?

Playground Games

Jacks

This is a very old game which can be played by one player or any number. It is also known as five stones.

Each player needs five small stones or pebbles and a bouncy ball. The pebbles are marked with a number from one to five on both sides, so that whichever way a pebble falls its number can be seen. Felt-tip pens are a good way of marking them.

Before play starts each player scatters his or her five stones on the ground. Then he or she tosses the ball in the air, bends down and picks up pebble 1 with the same hand as that which threw the ball before the ball bounces, after which the ball must be caught, as it is only allowed to bounce once. The pebble can be transferred from the ball-catching hand to the other one before or after the ball has been caught, but it must not still be in the throwing hand when the ball is thrown a second time.

Play continues in this way, with pebble 2 being picked up after the second throw of the ball, pebble 3 after the third, and so on until the player holds all five pebbles in his or her hand. If he or she drops a pebble, picks one up in the wrong order, or misses the ball after it has bounced once, then the player is out of the game.

The winner is the first player to complete the game without making a mistake. Players can play simultaneously or wait and take turns. With the latter arrangement it is easier to see if anyone cheats!

Traffic Lights

This is a team game which needs a fairly large space in which to play it. Players are divided into two teams, and one person does not join either team but becomes the Traffic Controller.

The Traffic Controller stands with his back to the two teams, who line up, one on each side of the play area, at the side furthest from the controller. The teams are 'traffic', whose job it is to move along imaginary roads, obeying the instructions called out by the controller.

At the beginning of the game the controller shouts 'green', and all the players start hopping towards him. Then the controller shouts 'amber', whereupon the players have to drop down on to their hands and knees and crawl.

After calling 'amber' the controller turns round and points to either of the two teams and shouts 'red'. At this point all the players in that team must freeze into position and not move. The controller can call 'red' to the other team as well, in which case they must follow the same procedure, or the controller can turn his back on the teams again and call out 'amber', allowing the players to proceed on all fours again, followed either by 'green', allowing them to hop, or 'red' again, which must be called out with the controller facing one team and pointing to it.

Anyone not on all fours after 'amber' is called, or anyone caught moving by the controller after he has called 'red' is out of the game.

The controller must follow the correct sequence of traffic lights — green, amber, red; red, amber, green, but the length of time for which the colour persists can be varied. The winner is the first person to reach the controller's end of the playground without disobeying the signals.

The White Spot

Any number of players can take part in this game. One of them needs a piece of chalk.

The player with the piece of chalk is called the Lord or Lady of the White Spot, and the other players have to try and touch the White Spot with out getting marked by the chalk. But at the same time, the Lord or Lady of the White Spot tries to mark the sleeves, backs or legs of the players with the chalk. If he or she succeeds, then the marked player becomes the Lord or Lady of the White Spot and the previous one joins the other players.

Jack, Jack, the Bread Burns

This is a fairly hectic game for any number of players. Two of the players are chosen to be the baker and his assistant, Jack. The others are the loaves in the oven.

The game starts with the baker shouting, 'Jack, Jack, the bread burns,' and he and his assistant rush to the 'loaves' and try to catch one. If they manage to do this the loaf is taken to the 'shop', part of the playground previously chosen as that area, where they have to sit down and not move. The loaves, of course, do their best not to be caught, which means that the baker and Jack have to try and catch them unawares. If on the other hand a loaf manages to catch the baker or Jack and prevent either of them from getting away, the one caught has to become a loaf themselves, and the loaf that caught them takes their place.

The game continues until either all the loaves have been taken to the shop, or until the baker and Jack have been caught and turned into loaves.

Questions, Questions, Questions!

Who?

1. Is the patron saint of Scotland?
2. Wrote *A Midsummer Night's Dream*?
3. Was the Roman god of war?
4. Was King Arthur's magician?
5. Was Odin?
6. Is said to have played the fiddle while Rome burned?
7. Plays the part of Michelle Holloway in *EastEnders*?
8. Wrote the Secret Seven stories?
9. Was president of the USA at the time of the Watergate crisis?
10. Painted the *Mona Lisa*?
11. Is leader of the Labour party?
12. Rode a horse naked through the streets of Coventry?
13. Is head of the Church of England?
14. First discovered penicillin?
15. Invented television?
16. Wrote stories about Pooh Bear?
17. First ran a mile in under four minutes?
18. Had a family home at Althorp?
19. Led the mutineers on the *Bounty*?
20. Discovered Australia?

Which?

1. Kind of fish is a kipper?
2. Kind of tree produces acorns?
3. Is the largest state of the USA?
4. Two countries are partly in Europe and partly in Asia?
5. Member of the Beatles was assassinated?
6. Sea parted to let Moses through?
7. Country has a rugby team called the Springboks?
8. Country has a maple leaf as its national emblem?
9. Metal is liquid under normal conditions?
10. Italian city is famous for its Bridge of Sighs?
11. Country has inhabitants called Walloons?
12. Author wrote *Pilgrim's Progress*?
13. British city was known as Auld Reekie?
14. Statue is in the middle of Piccadilly Circus in London?
15. Bird lays its eggs in other birds' nests?
16. Breed of cat has brilliant blue eyes?
17. Is the largest desert in the world?
18. Was the first city in the world to have an underground railway?
19. Country's flag has a rising sun on it?
20. Is larger, a UK pint or a US pint?

What?

1. Would you be able to do if you were bilingual?
2. Is the common name for sodium chloride?
3. Is measured in reams and quires?
4. Is a metronome?
5. Is campanology?
6. Is sold at London's New Covent Garden market?
7. Is the name of the long robe worn by Japanese women?
8. Was the name of the ship on which the Pilgrim Fathers sailed to America?
9. Are Orion, Cygnus and Leo?
10. Is the first day of Lent called?
11. Is an orthodontist?
12. Would you be able to do if you were ambidextrous?
13. Does the Beaufort Scale measure?
14. Does a pedometer measure?
15. Is Welsh Rarebit made from?
16. Is a pedigree?
17. Is a loganberry?
18. Is Stoke-on-Trent famous for?
19. Is a loggia?
20. Is silage?

Where?

1. Is Poets' Corner?
2. Is the Eiffel Tower?
3. Do pearls come from?
4. Does the Pope live?
5. In your body is your scapula?
6. Would you find a stamen?
7. Is the Road to the Isles?
8. Is the French town of St Tropez?
9. Would you buy things with roubles?
10. Is the Cape of Good Hope?
11. Would you find a lintel?
12. Might you see a sign depicting a pestle and mortar?
13. Would you find a bit, a browband and a curb chain?
14. Is the Great Barrier Reef?
15. Is Stonehenge?
16. Can you kiss the Blarney Stone?
17. Is the House of Keys?
18. Would you find a portcullis?
19. Would you see an aileron?
20. Is the Grand National run?

How Many?

1. Sides has a cube?
2. Pints are there in a quart?
3. Players are there in a cricket team?
4. Notes are there in an octave?
5. Gospels are there in the Bible?
6. Blackbirds were baked in a pie?
7. Sides has a pentagon?
8. Years has a decade?
9. Items are there in a gross?
10. Legs has a spider?
11. Hours are there in the month of March?
12. Wives had Henry VIII?
13. Pieces are there in a game of chess?
14. Thousands are there in a million?
15. Players are there in a game of tennis?
16. People are there in a jury?
17. Children has the Queen?
18. Acres are there in a square mile?
19. Centimetres are there in a foot, approximately?
20. Toes are there on a cat's back feet?

Silly Questions

1. What gets wetter the more it dries?
2. What do you lose every time you stand up?
3. What can you hold and not see?
4. What can you break without dropping it or hitting it?
5. What lives on itself but dies the moment it has devoured itself?

Quantity of Quaggas

Do you know what a quagga is, or was? It was a South African animal, related to the zebra, but with fewer stripes. Our artist has tried to draw a quagga, though she doesn't know what one looks like because she's never seen one, surrounded by lots of baby quaggas. Only one of the baby quaggas belongs to the mother quagga in the centre, and it is the one that is identical to the mother except in size. Which one is it?

R.S.V.P. *et al.*

Is this heading double Dutch to you, or do you know what it means? The letters are, of course, abbreviations, and not double Dutch at all, but standing for French and Latin words. As they are listed in some of the questions below, we're not going to reveal their meanings just yet!

English Abbreviations

What do these abbreviations stand for?

1. B.A.	5. F.A.	9. L.T.A.	13. O.H.M.S.	17. U.F.O.
2. B.B.C.	6. G.M.T.	10. M.B.E.	14. P.T.O.	18. V.A.T.
3. C.I.D.	7. H.M.S.O.	11. M.C.C.	15. R.N.	19. V.H.F.
4. C.O.D.	8. I.C.I.	12. N.S.P.C.C.	16. R.S.P.C.A.	20. Y.W.C.A.

Foreign Abbreviations

The following abbreviations are in everyday English use, but they stand for foreign, and usually Latin, words and phrases.

1. a.m.	5. *ibid.*	9. R.S.V.P.
2. e.g.	6. i.e.	10. viz.
3. *et al.*	7. N.B.	
4. etc.	8. p.m.	

Acronyms

The following abbreviations, which are pronounced as words, are called acronyms. What do they stand for?

1. Laser.	6. Quango.
2. N.A.L.G.O.	7. Quasar.
3. N.A.S.A.	8. Radar.
4. N.A.T.O.	9. U.N.O.
5. Oxfam.	10. U.N.E.S.C.O.

Jargon

Have you ever read a classified advertisement in a newspaper and been boggled by the abbreviations used to cut down the number of words? See if you can work out what the following mean.

1. Fr sle. Semi-det. 3-bed. bung., liv. rm., din. rm., kit., bath., sep. W.C., C.H., gd-sized gdn., gge. Nr. schools, stn., & shops.

2. Country hse htl. 12 beds., all H.&C.,6 baths., T.V. lnge., gd. home ckg., fab. vws.

3. Wtd., s/hnd typ. 120/60 w.p.m. Refs. req. Hrs. to suit.

Chemical Symbols

All the abbreviations below stand for chemical elements.

1. Ag.	5. Ca.	9. Fe.	13. K.	17. Pb.
2. Al.	6. Cl.	10. H.	14. Mg.	18. S.
3. Au.	7. Co.	11. Hg.	15. N.	19. Sn.
4. C.	8. Cu.	12. I.	16. O.	20. Zn.

Fifty Famous Riddles

How good are you at solving riddles? Here are some to test your brain. The answers are given at the back of the book, but don't give up too soon!

Adam
How might Adam have introduced himself to Eve, using three words that read the same forwards and backwards?

Angel
What did one angel say to another?

Auctioneer
What do you need to know to be an auctioneer?

Bed
When does a bed grow longer?

Bird
What bird can lift the most?

Boiled
What is boiled, then cooled, sweetened, then soured?

Break
What can you break without touching it?

Bus
What 'bus' crossed the ocean?

Cars
Where do cars get flat tyres?

Clock
Which part of a clock is always old?

Code
What code message is the same from left to right, from right to left, upside down and right side up?

Cows
Why do cows wear bells?

Dark
What is dark but made by light?

Dimple
What is a dimple?

Eat
In which month do people eat the least?

End
What always ends everything?

Farmer
What's the difference between a farmer and a dressmaker?

Garden
What runs round the garden without moving?

Heavy
Which is heavier, a kilo of lead or a kilo of feathers?

House
What is all over the house?

I
When is it correct to say 'I is'?

Instruments
What instruments do you carry in your ears?

Invention
What invention allows you to see through walls?

Ireland
If all Ireland should sink, what city would remain afloat?

Jam
Why did the jam roll?

Lengthened
What is lengthened by a cut at both ends?

London
Which part of London is in France?

Man
To whom does every man take off his hat?

Manicurist
Why was the manicurist so rich?

Mayonnaise
Why is mayonnaise never ready?

Months
How many months have twenty-eight days?

Music
What musical key makes a good army officer?

Net
When does a net hold water?

Noah
Where did Noah keep his bees?

Organist
What's the difference between an organist and a cold in the head?

P
Why is the letter P like a Roman emperor?

Penny
Why is a penny like a policeman?

Playing Cards
Why are playing cards like wolves?

Run
What can run but has no legs?

S
Why is the letter S like thunder?

Secrets
Why should you never tell secrets in a cornfield?

Sheep
Why do white sheep eat more than black sheep?

Sock
Why is it a mistake to put on a sock?

Tomorrow
What do we all put off until tomorrow?

Trees
What trees do fortune tellers like?

Vowels
Why is O the only vowel that is sounded?

Water
What can you add to a bucket of water to make it weigh less?

Westminster Abbey
Why is Westminster Abbey like a fireplace?

Word
What five-letter word has six left when you take two letters away?

Year
What day of the year is a command to go forward?

Racing Games

Thimble Race

You need an even number of players, preferably eight or more, a drinking straw for each player, and two thimbles.

Thimble Race is a team game for two teams of players. The teams line up in two rows, each player with a drinking straw in his or her mouth. Someone stands at the head of each team and places a thimble on the end of the leaders' straws. Then, on the word 'go', each leader has to turn to the player behind him and pass the thimble on to *their* straw without either player using their hands. In this way the thimble is passed down the line of players, and the first team to reach the last player wins. If, however, someone drops the thimble, it has to be passed back to the leader and the race started all over again.

Feather Race

As few as two players can participate in this race, or as many as twenty if you have a big room in which to run it. It is better played indoors than outdoors for reasons which will become obvious! Each player needs a feather and a paper plate.

The room needs a starting line and a finishing line, and the idea is that each contestant starts with a feather on a plate and races for the finish. The problem is, of course, keeping the feathers on the plates, as the players are not allowed to touch them by hand. If a feather is dropped then that player has to go back to the beginning and start again. The winner is the first person to cross the finishing line with his or her feather still on the plate.

Fish Race

Between two and six players can take part in this race. Each one will need a 'fish' cut out of a piece of paper, approximately 25 cm (10 in) long, and a rolled-up newspaper.

Again, a starting line and a finishing line are needed. The contestants place their fish with their tails touching the starting line, while they crouch behind with their newspapers. Then on the word 'go' each player wafts his or her newspaper behind the fish to propel it forwards towards the finishing line, and the first fish to cross the finishing line wins the race. The difficulty is to keep your fish moving in a straight line. If you are not very careful it will get entangled with someone else's fish and chaos will result!

Dressing-up Race

This again is a race for between two and six players. It requires lots of clothes of all shapes and sizes in which the players can dress up.

Contestants line up at one end of the room, each standing in front of a chair, or a chalk mark on the floor, if the game is being played in a room without a carpet. At the opposite end of the room, opposite each of the contestants, should be a pile of dressing-up clothes, with the same number of garments in each pile.

On the word 'go' each player rushes towards his or her pile of clothes, puts on one garment, and rushes back to the start, where they have to touch the chair or chalk mark

before haring off towards the pile of clothes again. They then have to put on another garment and rush back to the beginning. The race continues in this way, with each player only putting on one garment at a time, and going back to the start line after doing so. It is as well to have someone on hand to make sure there is no cheating! Clever players will soon realize that if they leave the difficult garments till last (the large pair of shoes, long skirt, etc.) then they will not trip over them as many times and are likely to have a better chance of winning the race. The race is won by the first person to arrive back at the starting line wearing all the clothes from his or her pile.

Snail's Race

This is a good race to hold after an exciting one like the dressing-up race. Two or more people can take part in it, and no equipment is needed.

Unlike any other kind of race you can imagine, the aim in the snail's race is not to be first to cross the finishing line, but last. But, and here is the difficult bit, everyone taking part *has* to keep moving forwards. Anyone who stops completely, or who moves backwards is eliminated.

Moving very, very slowly is a lot harder than it sounds, and the winner of the race will have completed a difficult task and really have earned their victory.

Signs and Ciphers

On this and the next three pages are some famous ciphers. Using them, can you decipher the messages on page 161?

Morse Code

A ● ▬	N ▬ ●	1 ● ▬ ▬ ▬ ▬
B ▬ ● ● ●	O ▬ ▬ ▬	2 ● ● ▬ ▬ ▬
C ▬ ● ▬ ●	P ● ▬ ▬ ●	3 ● ● ● ▬ ▬
D ▬ ● ●	Q ▬ ▬ ● ▬	4 ● ● ● ● ▬
E ●	R ● ▬ ●	5 ● ● ● ● ●
F ● ● ▬ ●	S ● ● ●	6 ▬ ● ● ● ●
G ▬ ▬ ●	T ▬	7 ▬ ▬ ● ● ●
H ● ● ● ●	U ● ● ▬	8 ▬ ▬ ▬ ● ●
I ● ●	V ● ● ● ▬	9 ▬ ▬ ▬ ▬ ●
J ● ▬ ▬ ▬	W ● ▬ ▬	0 ▬ ▬ ▬ ▬ ▬
K ▬ ● ▬	X ▬ ● ● ▬	
L ● ▬ ● ●	Y ▬ ● ▬ ▬	
M ▬ ▬	Z ▬ ▬ ● ●	

Semaphore

Rail Fence Cipher

In this cipher, the message is written out normally, and then alternate letters are lifted up and pushed down, to form two lines, and the message transcribed with first the upper line written down, and then the lower one. This is how it works. Assuming the message is CONTACT ARRIVES HEATHROW SATURDAY AFTERNOON. This would then be written out like this:

C N A T R I E H A H O S T R A A T R O N

O T C A R V S E T R W A U D Y F E N O

and transcribed like this:

C N A T R I E H A H O S T R A A T R O N O T C A R V S E T R W A U D Y F E N O .

It looks completely incomprehensible, but if you know the key it is quite easy to decipher. If you want to make deciphering easier, then you can put a point at the end of the top line; if you want to make it more difficult, then you can divide the letters up into mock words, like this:

CNAT RIEHAH OSTRAAT RONOT CARVSE TRWAUDY FENO.

Simple Alphabet Cipher

Real alphabet: A B C D E F G H I J K L M N O P Q R S T U V W X Y Z

Cipher alphabet: Z Y X W V U T S R Q P O N M L K J I H G F E D C B A

So the message   M E E T   X   A T   R A I L W A Y   S T A T I O N
would become: N V V G   C   Z G   I Z R O D Z B   H G Z G R L M

Column Cipher

The column cipher works in a similar way to the rail fence cipher, except that the letters of the message are written in two columns, either upwards or downwards. For example, the message SUSPECT KEN IS A SPY could be written like this:

S	E
U	N
S	I
P	S
E	A
C	S
T	P
K	Y

To create the cipher, you then write out the message in groups of letters reading across, like this:

S E U N S   I P S E A   C S T P K Y

The letters have been made into random groups to look like code words.

Null Cipher

The null cipher works by inserting meaningless letters, or 'nulls', either before or after each letter of the message. Any letters can be used as nulls. Take the message URGENTLY NEED NEW CODE BOOK. If you add a 'null' befor each of its letters, it might read like this:

B U J R L G P E K N X T B L W Y   V N K E P E L D   S N F E U W

B C N O Y D R E   L B K O B O J K

Double Dutch Cipher

The basis of the double Dutch cipher can be used to create hundreds of different ciphers. It consists of putting a meaningless syllable, such as AP, before every consonant in your message. So the message CHECK STAN'S ROOM FOR MICROFILM would read like this:

A P C A P H E A P C A P K   A P S A P T A A P N A P S

A P R O O A P M   A P F O A P R

A P M I A P C A P R O A P F I A P L A P M

You can change the syllable, and you can choose to put it after each consonant, or before or after each vowel, and thus create an enormous range of ciphers.

Number Cipher

A	B	C	D	E	F	G	H	I	J	K	L	M
1	2	3	4	5	6	7	8	9	10	11	12	13
N	O	P	Q	R	S	T	U	V	W	X	Y	Z
14	15	16	17	18	19	20	21	22	23	24	25	26

In this code WEDNESDAY MEETING CANCELLED would read:
23 5 4 14 5 19 4 1 25   13 5 5 20 9 14 7   3 1 14 3 5 12 12 5 4.

Crack a Code

Can you decipher these codes? They are based on the alphabets given on pages 157 to 160.

1. — — • • —   — • • • •   — • • —   — • • — • • — •

 — — — — —   • — — • • •   — • — •   — • —

 • • —   • — — •   • • • • —   • • — • • — — — — • • • • •

2. C E K E I S R U E S O C U S. H C C C L T O S R F R L E

3. I D F O I D L I D L O I D W   I D F I D R E I D D   O I D N
   I D T I D R I I D P   I D T O   I D T A I D D I D W O I D R I D T I D H

4.

5. 3 21 20 8 25 5 18 20   1 18 18 9 22 5 19   13 15 14 4 1 25   2 21 25
   15 14 9 15 14 19

6. T K A S K   T E O C C   O O D L   E L B E   O G O E

7.

8. H V M W   G V M   X S Z R I H   G L   X S V H G V I

9. 3 15 14 20 1 3 20   4 18 9 22 5 19   2 12 21 5   3 1 18

10. M B A K R J T Y H W A Z   M Y I S S S S J E N D W
    M K A X R J Y B S L   M N O C R P S F E V
    M D E P S R S Y A P G H E D

11. • • • •   — — — • — —   — — • — — • — — • — —

 • • — • • — • • • • —   • • •   — — —   — •

 — • • • —   — • • • •   — • • — — — — — •

12. P T A I O M   N A O L S N U   R D   O N O D Y   L Y O

13. O V Z E V   K Z X P Z T V   Z G   K Z W W R M T G L M

Solo Games

A collection of games to play on your own, using cards, dominoes and matchsticks or straws.

Clock Patience

This card game really does require patience, for although it does not involve any skill, it seldom works out as it should, which is why it is such fun to play.

All the cards are dealt out face down into thirteen piles, twelve of which are arranged like the numbers of a clock and the thirteenth of which is placed in the centre of the clock face. The object is to end up with four cards of the same rank in each pile at its correct place on the clock face. Four aces go at one o'clock, four twos at two o'clock, and so on, with the four jacks at eleven, the four queens at twelve and the four kings in the centre.

The game starts by the player taking the top card off the centre pile and looking at it. If it is, for example, a three, it is placed face up beside the three o'clock pile and the top card from that pile taken in its place. This card in turn is placed face up beside the appropriate pile, and the top card of that taken to be placed elsewhere, and so on. The game continues in this way until all the cards are in the correct places, but sometimes the player gets stuck when there are no more cards in a pile to be turned up. The only thing to do then is to shuffle the cards, deal them out again and hope for better luck in the next attempt.

Klondike

This is another, rather more complex, game of patience using playing cards.

Twenty-eight cards are dealt out in the following manner. First a row of seven is dealt, with the first card face up and the rest face down. Then a row of six is dealt, with the first card face up and overlapping the second card of the first row, and the rest of the cards face down and overlapping the other cards of the first row. Then a row of five cards is dealt in the same way, followed by four, three, two and one. As aces become available they are placed in a row above the rows dealt out, to become the foundations for the correct sequence of each suit to be built up from ace to king, which is the ultimate aim of the game.

The rest of the pack is placed face down and known as the 'stock'. Cards are turned up from the stock one at a time, and if they are not playable on the foundation aces or on the other cards laid out they are placed face up on a discard pile. The top card of the discard pile is always available to be played either on foundation aces or on the layout.

On the layout cards descending columns are built, of alternating colour, e.g. black nine on red ten, red eight on black nine, etc. Cards are turned up from the stock if none of the cards face up on the layout will fit. The bottom card of each sequence can be played on a foundation. A sequence as a whole may be transferred to another column to form a longer sequence. When a face-down card is exposed at the bottom of a column it is turned face up. When a complete column is cleared, the space may be only filled with a king or a sequence built on a king. The stock of cards may be played through once only. From the sequence, the suits are built up on the foundation aces.

Count Them Out

This is a dominoes game.

The dominoes are shuffled, and laid out in one line face downwards. They are then turned face up, without moving their positions in the line.

The player then begins by counting from 0 to 12, starting at the left-hand end of the line and moving his or her finger along the line of dominoes as he or she counts, touching a domino each time a number is said. When 12 is reached then the player starts again at 0, and when the end of the line of dominoes is reached then he or she goes back to the beginning again. Each time the pips on the domino being touched match the number being said (e.g. if the pips are four and five and the number being said is nine), the domino is pushed out of the line and the gap left closed up. The object is to discard all the dominoes.

Match Words

To play this game you will need twenty-eight matchsticks, or drinking straws, or even strips of paper.

The matchsticks should be arranged like this.

The object of the game is to see how many words you can make out of the matchsticks by removing a given number of sticks. You will find that removing less than five or more than eleven matches will not enable you to make many words, but lots can be made by removing numbers in between. Here are some examples.

Removing six matches

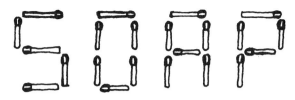

Removing seven matches

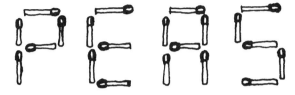

Removing eight matches

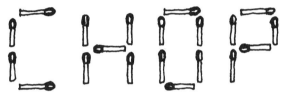

Removing nine matches

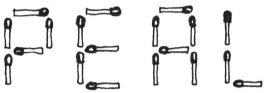

Removing ten matches

Matchless

Here's a trick to try with your matchsticks. Lay out six matchsticks, or straws, like this:

Now add five more to make nine!

Sporting Life

Thirty questions to test your knowledge of all kinds of sports.

1. What happens at Lords, Headingley and the Oval?
2. For which sport was Eddie Merckx famous?
3. What is the Fosbury Flop?
4. Who is 'Superbrat'?
5. What game do the Blades play?
6. What is Steve Cauthen's sport?
7. What does A.S.A. stand for?
8. Who was known as 'Mr Nasty'?
9. In which sport is the Londonderry Cup awarded?
10. What competes in the Fastnet Race?
11. In which sport do you 'bully off'?
12. In which Olympic Games did Princess Anne compete?
13. What is a 'duck'?
14. What game do the Chicago Bears play?
15. Where is the St Leger run?
16. Which sport might involve the butterfly?
17. Which sport takes place at Hickstead?
18. For which sporting event is Henley famous?
19. What do the New York Yankees play?
20. With which sport is Robin Cousins associated?
21. What takes place at the Rollerbury at Bury St Edmunds?
22. Who are the Bulls?
23. Who are the Minster Men?
24. Who is the 'Ice Maiden'?
25. What is Lucinda Green's great sporting triumph?
26. What is this unusual sport that is sometimes played in schools: EROSCALS?
27. What is Adrian Moorhouse's sport?
28. What is Sally Mapleson's sport?
29. In which sport would you use a crampon?
30. How many clubs are there in a set of golf clubs?

Sporting Trophies

Do you recognize these two famous cups?

1

2

Sports Bag

In which sports would you use this equipment?

1

2

3

4

5

6

7

8

9

10

Shadow Play

You can have a lot of fun making shadow shapes with your hands, and it is a skill that is quite easy to master. All you need is a blank wall, a darkened room, and a lamp or torch resting on a table.

The lamp or torch should be placed so that it shines on the wall, and your arm and hand should be positioned between the lamp and the wall, so that the shadows will be cast on the wall.

Here are some simple shapes you can make, but you will probably think of lots more you can make for yourself.

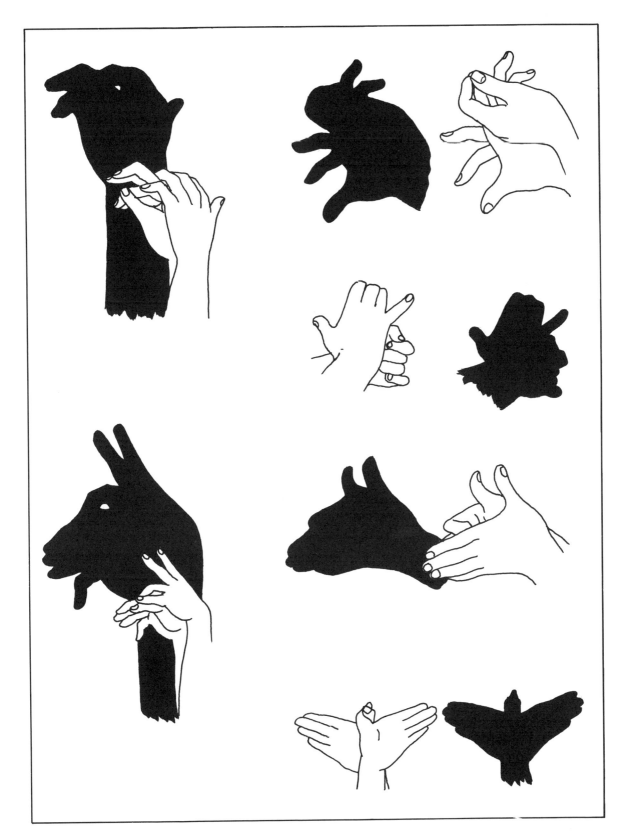

Spot the Difference

How many differences can you spot between these two pictures of people sailing? You should be able to find ten.

How many differences can you spot between these two skiing scenes? This time there are more than ten.

True or False?

Some of the extraordinary statements on these pages are true, and some are false. Can you spot which is which?

1. Turtles have no teeth.
2. There are twenty times as many sheep as people in New Zealand.
3. In Sicily people eat tulips in salads.
4. Water makes up two-thirds of our body weight.
5. There are more acres in Yorkshire than words in the Bible.
6. There is a reference to baseball in Jane Austen's novel *Northanger Abbey*, which was published in 1818.
7. Whist is a board game played with counters.
8. Papaya is a kind of parchment.
9. Bermuda has no surface streams or wells.
10. Some plants eat insects.
11. African elephants sleep standing up.
12. The word 'school' comes from a Greek word meaning 'leisure'.
13. Cats spend two-thirds of their lives asleep.
14. Spaniel dogs have six toes on their front feet.
15. A giraffe's neck contains the same number of bones as that of a man.
16. Chewing a stick is a good way to clean your teeth.

17. There is a place called Hell in Norway.

18. It is impossible to sneeze and keep your eyes open at the same time.

19. Charles Dickens wrote the novel *Far From the Madding Crowd*.

20. Dogs sweat through their paws.

21. The first modern Olympic Games were held in Athens in 1956.

22. Babies can breathe and swallow at the same time.

23. Saudi Arabia imports camels and sand.

24. Robert Louis Stevenson produced the world's first steam locomotive.

25. Mary, Queen of Scots played billiards.

26. Venice's canals have at least one set of traffic lights.

27. The Panama Canal connects the Mediterranean Sea with the Red Sea.

28. The safety pin was invented in the Mediterranean area in the Bronze Age.

29. Benjamin Franklin invented the digital clock in 1777.

30. A tonne of coal is needed to produce a tonne of paper.

31. Twenty-five different dialects are spoken in India.

32. Mosquitoes prefer biting blond people.

33. Eskimos use fridges to stop their food from freezing.

34. The Eiffel Tower is the world's tallest building.

35. Cows have four stomachs.

36. An earwig is a kind of judge's wig with flaps.

37. Britain's first motorway was opened in 1949.

38. The bark of the willow tree contains aspirin.

39. Whisky is made from fermented turnips.

40. A caterpillar has nearly four times as many muscles as a man.

Teasing Tricks I

If you've ever fancied yourself as a magician, here are some tricks to try out on your friends. Practise them first to make sure you can do them without anyone spotting you.

Pushing a Coin Through a Solid Table

The trick

Ask someone in the audience to lend you two coins, asking them to make a note of the coins' dates before passing them over. Sit at the table, and place the coins several feet apart on the table 'so every one can see there is no trickery involved' and pick up one coin in your right hand and one in your left hand. Put your left fist under the table and your right fist on top of the table. You now press your right fist down hard on the table 'to push the coin through the table'. A clink is heard! You then show that your right fist is empty, and you bring your left fist from under the table and open it to reveal two coins. You have pushed a coin through a solid table! You hand the coins back to the member of the audience who lent them to you, asking them to check that the dates on the coins are the same, which, of course, they are.

The secret

When you place the coins on the table you put the right-hand one near the edge of the table nearest to you. You pick up the other coin in your left hand and at the same time push the right-hand coin off the table into your lap with your right hand. Your right fist (now empty) then rests on the table, while your left fist picks up the other coin from your lap. At the time when the right fist is meant to be pushing the coin through the table you clink the two coins together in your left fist to add a touch of realism. If you practise the trick a few times you should be able to do it without anyone spotting the deception.

Open, Sesame!

This is a card trick. It requires one pack of cards and a few grains of salt.

The trick

Ask someone in the audience to shuffle the cards, cut them (i.e. divide them into two piles) and place them in two separate piles on the table. Ask the volunteer to pick up any card from the first pile, memorize it, and replace it on the top of the second pile. Then ask him or her to place the first pile on top of the second pile, straighten the pack, and leave the cards face upwards on the table. You then tap the side of the pack with a pen or pencil, say, 'Open, sesame!' and the cards will separate to reveal the card the volunteer chose.

The secret

You prepare yourself by having a few grains of salt between your thumb and forefinger. When you tell the volunteer to replace the card on the top of the second pile you tap the pile to indicate it, dropping the salt on the cards as you do so. When the pack is turned face upwards the salt will be between the chosen card and those above it, and when the side of the pack is tapped the cards will naturally separate at this point.

The Magic Matchstick

For this trick you will need two matchsticks and a man's handkerchief.

The trick

Ask someone in the audience to pass you a matchstick, marked in some way so he or she will recognize it again. Place the match in the centre of a handkerchief and fold the handkerchief over it. Hold out the folded hanky to the volunteer, asking him to feel that the match is there, and to break it in half. Then open the handkerchief to reveal the match, unbroken, and give it back to the volunteer.

The secret

The handkerchief you use has a second matchstick concealed in one of its hems. With the handkerchief carefully folded, you make sure it is this match that the volunteer feels and snaps in half, while his match remains in the part of the handkerchief you hold in your hand. When the match has been restored to the volunteer, you put your handkerchief away in your pocket. It is as well to have a second handkerchief, identical to the first, ready in your pocket should anyone ask to examine it to see how you did the trick.

Find the Coin

For this trick you need a coin and a blindfold.

The trick

Ask for the help of three members of the audience. One of them blindfolds you, and then you invite any one of the three to pick up a coin which you have placed on the table. They can use either hand to pick up the coin, but when they have picked it up they have to hold the hand containing it pressed firmly to their forehead, in order that they might concentrate on the coin, thus enabling you, by telepathy, to ascertain which person is holding the coin.

You then tell all three to hold their fists out in front of them, and you remove the blindfold, immediately telling the audience which one is holding the coin, and which fist it is in!

The secret

The person who was holding the coin to his forehead will have one hand paler than the other if you wait about half a minute before asking him to take his fist away from his head. You can thus instantly tell not only which person had the coin, but in which hand it was held!

Raising the Ice

For this trick you will need an ice cube, a cup of water, a piece of string and some salt.

The trick

This is a very impressive and seemingly impossible trick. All you have to do is to lift an ice cube out of a cup of water with a piece of string!

The secret

If you challenge someone to do this they will probably spend many frustrating minutes trying to tie the string round the ice cube, but the answer is much more simple. All you do is lay the end of the string on top of the ice cube and sprinkle some salt over it. Leave it for a minute or two, and then try lifting the string. The ice cube will be safely attached to the other end!

Why does this happen? Well, the salt melts the ice initially, but then the lower temperature of the ice cube freezes the melted area again, and the string becomes frozen on the ice cube, enabling you to lift it out of the water.

Telegrams

Telegrams

This game can be played by almost any number of players. Each will need a piece of paper and a pencil.

The game starts by each player calling out a letter of the alphabet, round and round until a dozen letters have been called out. The players write down all the letters called out in order. Their job then is to write an amusing telegram, using the letters as the first letters of each word in the message, in the order in which they were read out. For example, the letters might be H, A, S, I, T, D, O, H, W, B, S, I, O. Telegrams which could be made from them could be:

> HAD ACCIDENT SKIING. INJURED TOE. DECIDED ON HOLIDAY WITH BOAT, SAILING INDIAN OCEAN.

> HAROLD ARRIVED SAFELY IN TEXAS. DIGGING OILWELLS HAPPILY. WILL BEN SELL IRISH OIL?

The winner is the writer of the telegram considered by everyone to be the most amusing.

Tastebud Test

Tastebud Test

This is an amusing game for parties or winter afternoons. All it needs is a number of cups, mugs or saucers, as many teaspoons and blindfolds as there are participants, and someone who isn't playing to prepare a number of beverages. The idea, you see, is for each blindfolded player to taste a spoonful of the contents of each cup, mug or saucer, and say what it is.

Here are some things that might be put in the cups: tea, coffee (with milk and without), cocoa, apple juice, orange squash, lemon squash, lime juice, lemonade, fizzy mineral water, soda water, tap water, cold gravy, cold soup of various sorts, and so on.

The player who makes the greatest number of correct guesses wins.

Tree Time

If you rearrange each set of numbered leaves you will find that the letters spell out the names of thirteen trees which can be fitted into the crossword grid.

ACROSS

DOWN

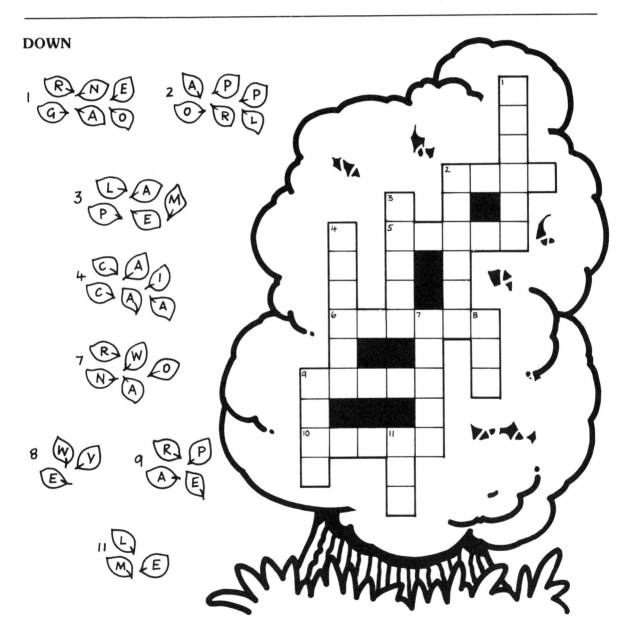

Teasing Tricks II

Naughty tricks to play on unsuspecting friends.

Green Bath

This is a good trick to play on an older sister, especially if she is getting ready to go out. All you need is some green food colouring, which you will probably find in the kitchen, or which can be bought quite cheaply from a grocer's shop or supermarket.

Pretend to be feeling especially kind and helpful towards your brother or sister, but don't overdo it or they may become suspicious! When they are flapping around looking for their clean clothes to get ready to go out, offer to run them a nice hot bath, to save them time. They will be delighted! Then all you do is put a few drops of the food colouring in the water, give it a swirl round, and wait for the scream. It's as well to be prepared to make a quick getaway at this stage!

Finger Language

For this trick you need an unsuspecting victim and a table.

Get your victim to hold his or her hand so that the first three fingers can rest flat on the table and the thumb and little finger are tucked out of the way, as shown in the drawing. Say, 'I'm going to teach you to speak with your fingers. It's very simple, really. All you do is wiggle a finger for "yes", and lift a finger off the table for "no", in answer to my three questions. You must answer the first question with your index finger, the second question with your middle finger, and the third question with your ring finger.'

Your victim will be relieved that it all sounds so simple and harmless, and will readily agree.

You are now ready to ask your questions. Let us suppose your victim's name is Ben.

Ask him the first question. 'Is your name Ben?' He will wiggle his first finger to answer 'yes'.

Ask him the second question. 'Are you happy today?' He may either wiggle his second finger to answer 'yes', or lift it off the table to answer 'no'.

Ask him the third question. 'Are you a silly idiot?' Poor Ben will want to answer 'no', but he will find he is quite unable to lift his ring finger by itself off the table in order to do so. His struggles will be interpreted as wiggling the finger to answer 'yes', and he will suddenly know what you are up to!

Getting the Tangue All Tongueled Up

Whether you are on your own or with a group of friends you can have a great time trying out these tongue-twisters.

If there is a group of you, pick a tongue-twister each and get one member of the party ready with a watch. Then see who can repeat their twister for one minute without getting it wrong.

You may like to make up some twisters of your own, but here are some to start you off.

That bloke's back brake-block's broke.

Red lorry. Yellow lorry.

Around the rugged rock the ragged rascal ran.

Three hundred and thirty-six thirsty soldiers sifted thistles in the thistle field.

The sixth sheikh's sixth sheep's sick.

Can you imagine an imaginary menagerie manager imagining managing an imaginary menagerie?

The new nuns knew the true nuns knew the new nuns too.

Thin sticks. Thick bricks.

Sheila says she sells sea-shells by the sea shore.

Adam and aunt were adamant Adam hadn't added Adam's aunt.

The black-backed bath brush.

The cruel ghoul's cool gruel.

Shall Sarah Silling share her silver shilling?

Many an anemone knows an enemy anemone.

A slattern in a shawl shovelled soft snow slowly.

Bring back British 'Back Britain' brooches.

The short sort shoot straight through.

The sun shines on shop signs.

Fifty shabby pheasant shooters had a pleasant shoot.

A truly rural frugal ruler's mural.

Tangram Teasers

A tangram is an ancient Chinese puzzle consisting of seven pieces, all of which are cut out of a single square as shown below. Tangrams can be bought, or they can be made by cutting them out of card or paper. They can then be used to construct various forms and shapes, as shown on these two pages.

If you wish to make your own tangram, then trace off the shape given. If you wish to make yours smaller, you have to bear in mind that the medium-sized triangle, the square and the rhomboid are all twice the area of one of the smaller triangles. Each of the large triangles is four times the area of one of the small triangles. All the angles of the pieces are either right angles, 45° angles or 135° angles.

Having acquired a tangram, try to arrange the pieces to make the shapes shown. It's not easy!

Unusual Objects

All the things on these two pages are quite ordinary, but they have been drawn from unusual angles, and are not to scale. How many do you recognize?

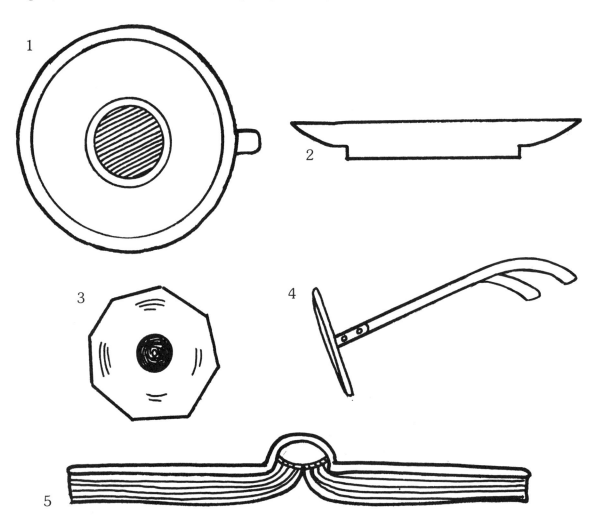

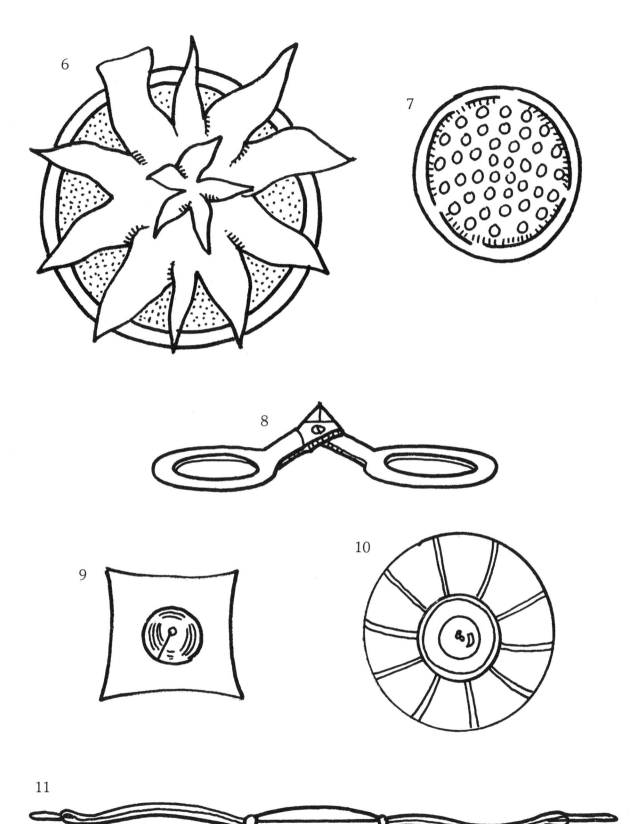

6

7

8

9

10

11

Games for When You're Unwell

My House

If you are confined to bed for a number of days, and are well enough to feel bored, you will have an enjoyable time playing My House. You will need someone to bring you a scrapbook, some old magazines or catalogues, a pair of scissors, and some paste.

The idea is to plan your ideal house, which may be based on the house in which you live now, or may be imaginary. On one page of the scrap book you draw a floor plan of one room of the house, say the living-room, and on the opposite page you stick cut-out pieces of furniture, curtains, and so on which will go in that room. It's a good idea to stick them with something that's not too permanent, so that if you find a nicer piece of furniture you can use it instead of the first one you saw.

Room by room you work your way through the house, not forgetting the bathroom and kitchen. If you like you can add outbuildings, say a garage, with a picture of the kind of car you would like to see in it, and so on. You may well enjoy the game so much that you continue the project when you are up and about again.

Where Am I?

This game requires the help of a visitor, but does not need any equipment.

The patient thinks of a place and an activity that could be done in that place, and the other person, by means of twenty questions which can only be answered by 'yes' or 'no' has to guess where the person is and what he or she is doing. For example, the player might decide that are at Wembley playing in the FA Cup Final, at Dover preparing to swim the Channel, at Buckingham Palace, waiting to receive an honour from the Queen, or anywhere else they would like to imagine.

If the other player fails to guess the answer after twenty questions, then the first player can have another go, but if they do guess it, it is their turn to think of a place and an activity.

Name Message

This game is played by the patient alone. He or she will need a piece of paper and a pencil.

The player writes a name, preferably their own name, down the left-hand side of the paper, and then writes the name in reverse down the right-hand side of the paper. So if your name is ANNE, it would look something like this:

```
A                    E
N                    N
N                    N
E                    A
```

Then, allowing as many minutes as there are letters in the name, the idea is to write messages that start and end with the letters on either side of the page. ANNE has four letters, so there would be four minutes in which to write the messages, which might be something like this:

Angela, please go home at oncE.

Never run upstairs when wearing a long gowN.

Neither Fred nor Ted was iN.

Eventually I can expect to hear from EvA.

The sentences can be anything at all, as long as they make sense and fit between the letters. Having tried the game with one name, a player can then try out the names of some of his or her friends.

Concentration

This game can be played by one person or by any number. Pencils and paper are needed, together with a page from a magazine which is crammed with facts and/or pictures.

Each player studies the page for two minutes (you have to time yourself), then puts it out of sight and writes down everything they can remember about the page. If several people are playing then each player waits his or her turn to have a go. At the end, the person with the longest correct list of things wins. If only one person is playing then he or she must check the page at the end to see how many things were remembered correctly.

Word Links

This is a really good game for two people, but it could be played by one if they have a pencil and a piece of paper with which to note down the words that are produced.

A general topic is thought up — say names of animals, or countries, and the first player says an example. Let us suppose it is 'horse'. The second player then has to think of another example that begins with the last letter of the previous word. So he or she might say 'elephant'. The first player then has to think of an animal beginning with T, which might be 'tapir', and the second player might then counter with 'rabbit'. So the game continues, until either one player becomes stuck for a word or repeats a word that has already been said. When this happens the other player wins.

If someone is playing it alone they can simply write down the words in a long list until they get stuck. Then it's time to choose another subject, or another game!

Umbrellas Galore!

Each umbrella contains a word connected with bad weather with the letters jumbled up. Unjumble the letters and fit the words in the grid.

184

Ulna and Others

The ulna is a bone in the human body, as are all the other words shown below. Do you know whereabouts in the body each one is situated? See if you can match the numbered bones with those spelt out.

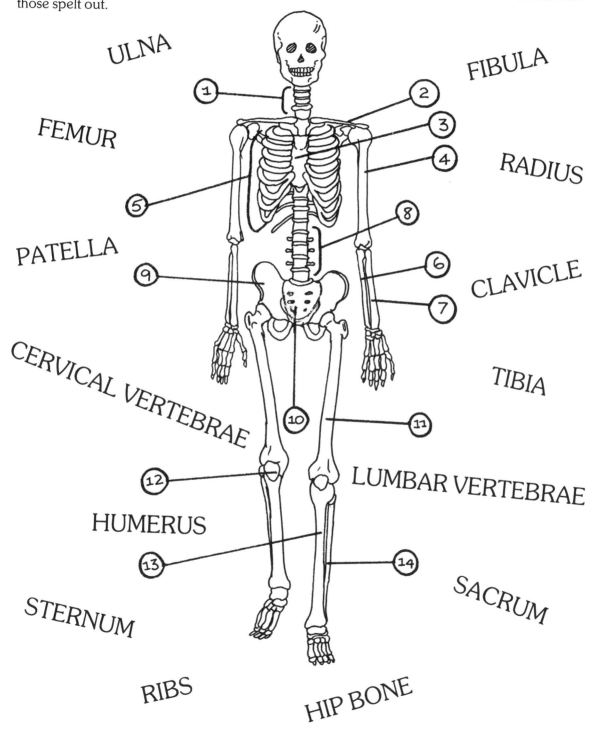

ULNA

FIBULA

FEMUR

RADIUS

PATELLA

CLAVICLE

CERVICAL VERTEBRAE

TIBIA

LUMBAR VERTEBRAE

HUMERUS

SACRUM

STERNUM

RIBS

HIP BONE

Visual Feast

Eye Test

Have a look at this staircase. Which is the top
step, and which is the bottom step?

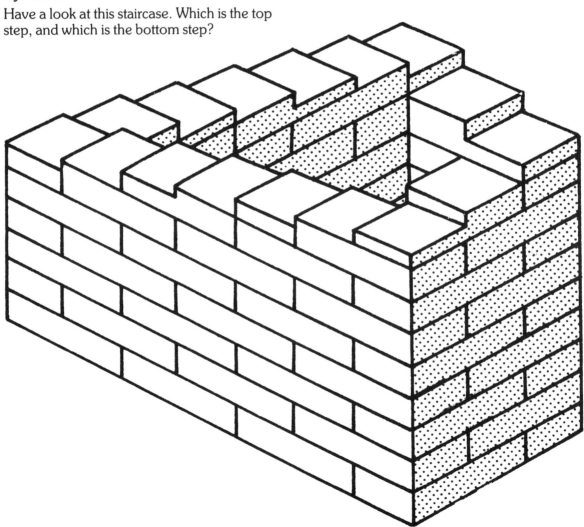

Triangle Test

Could this simple triangle be made easily?

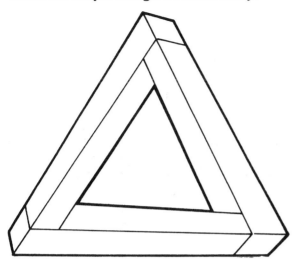

Crazy Object

If you were a skilled carpenter, could you make this object?

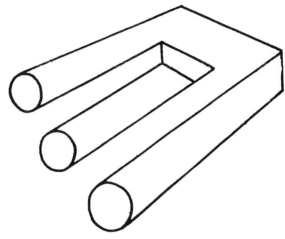

Lining Up

Which centre line is longer, A or B?

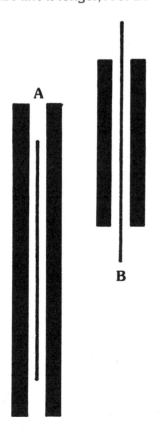

Sign Language

In each of these squares is a plus sign, a minus sign, a multiplication sign and a division sign. One square is a bit different from all the others. Which is it, and what is different about it?

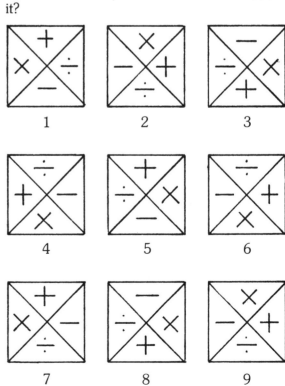

Parallels Problem

Which of these twelve horizontal lines are parallel with each other, and which are not?

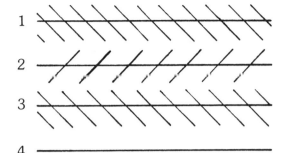
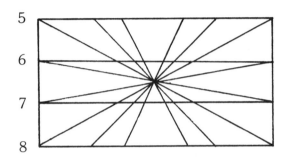

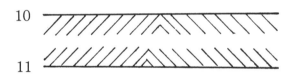

What's This?

Is it a message — or what?

Seeing Spots

Concentrate on these black squares for a minute or two. Do you start to see black spots at the junctions of the white lines?

Try drawing the grid on plain paper, and colouring in the squares and repeating the experiment. If you colour the squares blue you are likely to see orange spots; if you colour them red you will see green spots. What happens if you colour them green?

Star and Stripes

Look at the upper drawing below, and keep your eyes fixed on the centre star while you are counting slowly up to 100. Then look at the lower drawing. The lines curve in the opposite direction!

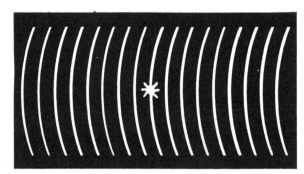

188

Round in Circles I

Which circle is the larger, that inside the square or that outside it?

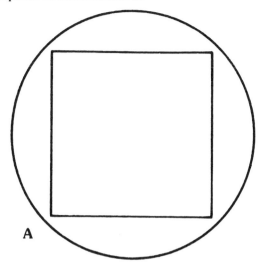

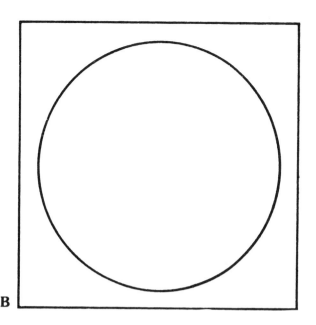

Round in Circles II

Study this large black and white circle, and as you are doing so turn this book round as fast as you can so it is spinning on the table like a record on a turntable. Then stop and look at the circle again. Is it now moving round in the opposite direction?

Angled Question

Which line is the longer, that from A to C or that from B to D?

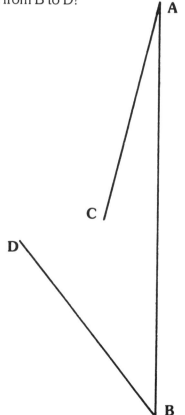

Cube Conundrum

Study this cube for a minute or so and see what happens. It should turn itself over!

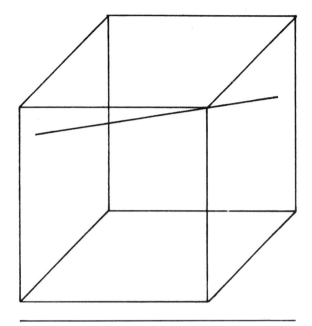

A Matter of Distance

Which distance is the greater — that between A and B or that between B and C?

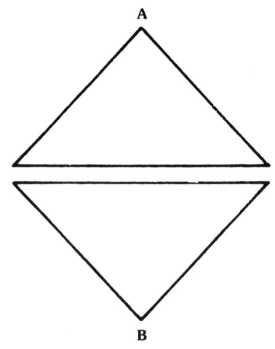

Pentangles

How many triangles are there in this pentagon?

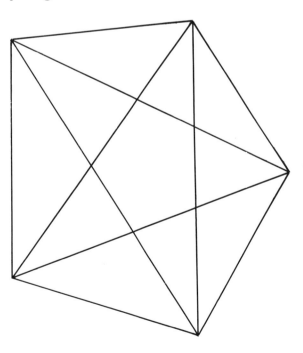

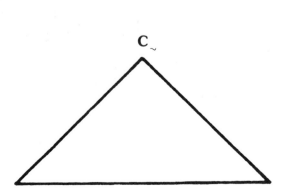

Verse and Worse

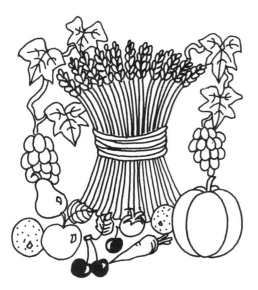

Famous Lines

Can you identify the poems from which these famous lines are taken, and say who wrote them?

1. 'Shall I compare thee to a summer's day?
   Thou art more lovely and more temperate:'
2. 'She walks in beauty, like the night
   Of cloudless climes and starry skies:'
3. 'Wee, sleekit, cowrin', tim'rous beastie,
   O, what a panic's in thy breastie!'
4. 'Hail to thee, blithe Spirit!
   Bird thou never wert,'
5. 'Season of mists and mellow fruitfulness,
   Close bosom-friend of the maturing sun;'
6. 'What is this life if, full of care,
   We have no time to stand and stare.'
7. 'The splendour falls on castle walls
   And snowy summits old in story:'
8. 'A garden is a lovesome thing, God wot!'

Poets Laureate

Which of the following poets **have not** held the office of Poet Laureate?

Ben Jonson, William Wordsworth, John Keats, John Masefield, Cecil Day Lewis, Philip Larkin, John Betjeman, Ted Hughes.

Hidden Fruits

Hidden in this verse are thirteen different fruits. Can you spot them all? The first one has been shown in bold type as an example.

Ah! I**f I g**et my good ship home
I'll find a tempting rural spot,
Where mayhap pleasant flowers will bloom,
And there I'll shape a charming cot.

Where bees sip nectar in each flower,
And Philomel on hawthorn rests,
I'll shape a rustic, sun-kissed bower —
A bower meet for angel guests.

Then she who lives and loves with me,
Full snug our days of calm repose,
Sole monarch of the flowers will be —
For Myra is indeed a rose.

Vision On

Silver Screen Twenty Questions

Test your knowledge of the film world.

1. What kind of animals was *Born Free* about?
2. Who played eight roles in *Kind Hearts and Coronets*?
3. What was the name of the dreadful girls' school about which many films were made?
4. Who fought his way through the West for a fistful of dollars?
5. Which American composer did Cary Grant play in *Night and Day*?
6. Who was the Godfather?
7. When was Mickey Mouse born — 1928, 1938 or 1948?
8. What was the name of Roy Rogers's horse?
9. Which Ken Russell film concerns the writing of a story by Mary Shelley, and who was the most famous screen player of the character Mary Shelley created?
10. Who played Maria von Trapp, and what was the name of the film about her?

11. In which Charlie Chaplin film did Charlie cook his shoes?
12. In which film did Gene Kelly dance in a downpour?
13. Who was the original Shane?
14. Who played Gandhi?
15. Who came to stardom playing Harry Palmer in *The Ipcress File*?
16. What connects *Bananas* with *The Purple Rose of Cairo*?
17. In which film did Clark Gable star as Rhett Butler?
18. The musical *High Society* has been brought back to the London stage. On which 1940 film was it based?
19. On whose novel is *A Room With A View* based?
20. Which 1987 film is based on correspondence between an American writer and a London bookseller?

Small Screen Twenty Questions

Test your knowledge of the TV world.

1. Who presents *Mastermind*?
2. What is the name of Postman Pat's village?
3. Which 'round' did John Craven make famous?
4. Where is Pebble Mill?
5. Who is John Altman better known as?
6. Who invites viewers to call his bluff?
7. Whose pet is Emu?
8. Who says, 'Nick, nick, nick'?
9. Who is TV-am's exercise queen?
10. What's the name of Roland Rat's animal friend?

11. Who played Agatha Christie's elderly lady detective in the recent *Miss Marple* series?
12. Which glamorous role was played by Linda Evans?
13. Who was Sir Humphrey Appleby?
14. What is the name of the store in *Are You Being Served*?
15. Who is addressed as 'Please, Sir'?
16. Who starred in the TV version of *The Secret Diary of Adrian Mole Aged 13¾*?
17. What is Dame Edna Everage's real name?
18. Who made and presented *Life on Earth*?
19. Who says, 'May your God go with you'?
20. Which children's programme is named after a flag?

Famous Faces

Whose are these famous faces from the small screen?

1

2

3

4

5

6

7

8

Games for the Very Young

The games in this section are specially chosen for three-, four-, five- and six-year-olds.

The Farmer's in His Den

Any number of players can take part in this game. One player is the farmer, and he or she stands in the middle of a circle formed by the other players standing round holding hands. The circle walks round the farmer singing the following verses:

> The farmer's in his den
> The farmer's in his den
> Heigh-ho, heigh-ho
> The farmer's in his den.
>
> The farmer wants a wife
> The farmer wants a wife
> Heigh-ho, heigh-ho
> The farmer wants a wife.

At this point in the song the circling players stop, and the farmer chooses one of them as his wife, and this player joins the farmer in the centre of the circle. The players in the circle join hands again, and walk round again, singing the next verse:

> The wife wants a child
> The wife wants a child
> Heigh-ho, heigh-ho
> The wife wants a child.

The circle stops again, and this time the farmer's wife chooses one of the players to be her child. This player joins her and the farmer in the centre while the circle joins hands again and starts walking round and singing the next verse:

> The child wants a nurse
> The child wants a nurse
> Heigh-ho, heigh-ho
> The child wants a nurse.

And so the circle stops again, and the child chooses a player to be the nurse and join them in the centre. The circle re-forms and sings the next verse:

> The nurse wants a dog
> The nurse wants a dog
> Heigh-ho, heigh-ho
> The nurse wants a dog.

The nurse chooses a dog and then every one sings the last verse:

> We all pat the dog
> We all pat the dog
> Heigh-ho, heigh-ho
> We all pat the dog.

Every one then pats the dog, preferably not too roughly, and the player who was the dog becomes the farmer for the next round.

Pat-a-Cake

This is another singing game for any number of players. It is best to have an adult or an older child to lead the singing and demonstrate the actions. This person stands facing the other players.

After running through the words of the song briefly, the leader starts the players off singing the words and doing the actions, which are as follows:

Pat-a-cake, pat-a-cake, baker's man

Clap your hands

Bake me a cake as fast as you can

Roll out the dough and put it in a mould

Pat it and prick it and mark it with 'B'

Pat the cake, prick it with an imaginary fork, and write a B in the air with one finger

And bake it in the oven for baby and me.

Place the cake in the oven and close the oven door.

Choo-Choo Tag

This is a game for any odd number of players. One is chosen as the guard and the rest form pairs.

The pairs form an engine and a coach, the coach holding the engine round the waist as they chug round the room like a little train. All the trains thus formed go round the room like this, all trying to keep out of the way of the guard, who is trying to catch a train. This is done by catching a 'coach' player round the waist. If the guard manages to do this, the engine of that train drops out and becomes the guard in the next round of the game.

Three Blind Mice

Any number of players can take part in this game. It requires one player to be the farmer's wife. He or she stands in the middle of a circle of players, who join hands, dance round and sing:

Three blind mice,
Three blind mice,
See how they run,
See how they run.

They all run after the farmer's wife
Who cut off their tails with a carving knife.
Did you ever see such a sight in your life
As three blind mice?

As the last word 'mice' is sung, the children let go of each other's hands and run as fast as they can to their 'hole' or place of safety agreed beforehand, such as touching a wall or a sofa. The farmer's wife has to try and catch one of the players before he or she reaches the 'hole', and any mouse so caught becomes the farmer's wife in the next round.

Jump To It

This is a jumping game which young children will greatly enjoy. You need two markers about a metre (3 ft) long, such as lengths of wood, tape or rope.

Start with the markers about 5 cm (2 in) apart. *Everyone* can jump over that! When each player has had a go, widen the markers slightly and let them jump again. The game continues in this way until the Great Divide becomes so wide that no one can jump it. The winner is the last player to jump it successfully.

Vroom, Vroom

How many differences are there between these two pictures of a souped-up hot rod?

Voice Over

Trace the note the player blows through this amazing musical instrument.

Word Play

Cat-ch-words

Fill in the blanks to make words that match the definitions given.

1. Propulsive device	C A T — — — — —
2. Disperse	— C A T — — —
3. Involved	— — — — — C A T —
4. Twin-hulled boat	C A T — — — — — —
5. Waterfall	C A T — — — — —
6. Calamity	C A T — — — — — — —
7. Place	— — C A T —
8. Olympic event	— — C A T — — — —
9. Garden tools	— — C A T — — — —
10. Leave empty	— — C A T —

A Man's Rag

'A man's rag' is an anagram of the word 'anagrams'. And an anagram is a word or words made from the letters of another word or words. Find single words for each of the anagrams below.

1. NINE THUMPS
2. SEA TERM
3. ILL-FED
4. LIFE'S AIM
5. SEEN AS MIST
6. MADE SURE
7. A STEW, SIR
8. REAL FUN
9. A CUTE CALL
10. DAN TIES IT ON

Add An S?

Do you know how to form the plurals of the following words?

1. Cargo.
2. Oboe.
3. Opera.
4. Mother-in-law.
5. Potato.
6. Salmon.
7. Ox.
8. Crisis.
9. Medium.
10. Teaspoonful.

Male and Female

Do you know the feminine forms of these words?

1. Baron.
2. Boar.
3. Cob.
4. Drake.
5. Earl.
6. Gander.
7. Marquis.
8. Peacock.
9. Ram.
10. Tom (cat).

Boys and Girls

Each of the words below can be completed by the addition of a boy's name or a girl's name in the blank spaces. Can you spot which names are needed?

1. ARM ___.
2. SUL ___.
3. ___ ERNAL.
4. SUM ____.
5. ___ BIN.
6. DIL ____.
7. PEN ___.
8. HAR _____.
9. SPH ____ AL.
10. A ____ BLE.

Spelling Bee

How many of the following words are spelt correctly?

1. Cooly.
2. Deisel.
3. Flourescence.
4. Gorrilla.
5. Manageable.
6. Mantlepiece.
7. Parallel.
8. Rythm.
9. Separate.
10. Threshold.

Word Games I

Animal, Vegetable, Mineral

Any number of people can play Animal, Vegetable, Mineral, which is a guessing game in which a subject is decided upon by one player while the others try to guess what it is.

One player chooses a subject word. Let us suppose it is 'apple tree'. The first question to be asked would be 'Animal, vegetable or mineral?', and this is the only question which can be answered with a word other than 'yes' or 'no'. In the case of the subject 'apple tree', the answer would be 'vegetable', since it is a plant that grows.

Having determined in which category the subject lies, the players can fire questions thick and fast at the person who has chosen the subject, but he or she will only answer 'yes' or 'no'. So, for example, if asked 'Does it grow in this country?' the player would answer 'Yes', but if asked 'Where does it grow?' the player would not be able to answer.

Players can either decide to have a limit on the number of questions asked, or a time limit

for questioning, or may just go on until the subject is guessed. The player who guesses correctly then becomes the one to choose a subject.

A Was an Apple Pie

This word game can be played by any number of players who sit round in a circle. They have to name verbs beginning with successive letters of the alphabet, starting with A, and can agree to leave out awkward letters such as Q, X and Z.

Play begins with the first player saying, 'A was an apple pie. A ate it,' or another verb beginning with A. The next player then says, 'B borrowed it,' or another verb beginning with B. The third player then says, 'C curried it,', and the fourth says, 'D drew it', and so it goes on through the alphabet. There is no need to repeat the words 'A was an apple pie' each time, but if the game continues for a second round verbs that have already been used cannot be repeated.

Just a Minute

This game requires a stop watch, or a watch with a second hand, and an impartial 'judge' to see fair play.

The idea is that players talk for exactly one minute on a given topic. This is not as easy as it sounds! Topics chosen might be: The Best Birthday I've Ever Had, Going on Holiday, The Street Where I Live, A Visit to the Theatre, and so on. Each player starts with ten points, and if they manage to speak on their topic for sixty seconds without hesitating, repeating themselves or deviating from the point, they are awarded another five points. If, however, they do commit any of these faults, they lose two points. The winner is the person who finishes with the greatest number of points. If there is a tie, then the two players can have another go on another topic — possibly one that is a little more difficult.

Coffee Pot

This game can be played by any number of people. One player thinks of a word that has two meanings, or of two words that are spelt differently and have different meanings, such as 'here' and 'hear'. He or she then has to say aloud a sentence using both meanings, but substituting the words 'coffee pot' for the chosen words. For example, if the chosen words were 'here' and 'hear', the player might say, 'I couldn't coffee pot the birds as I was passing coffee pot yesterday.'

Each of the other players may then ask one question, to which the first player must reply using one or the other of the chosen words, or the chosen word in either of its meanings, but again disguised as 'coffee pot'.

It is the objective of the other players to guess the chosen word or words, and the one that does so scores a point. But if the word is not guessed then the player who thought it up scores a point.

Players take it in turns to think of 'coffee pot' words, and when everyone has had a turn the player with the greatest number of points wins.

Botticelli

This is another speaking game which can be played by any number of players.

One player thinks of the name of a famous person or well-known fictional character, and tells the other players the initial letter of the character's surname.

The other players then ask a series of 'indirect' questions to which the first player must give a suitable reply. For example, let us suppose that player A has chosen the actor Michael Caine as his subject.

> Player B: Are you a singer?
> Player A: No, I am not Caruso.
> Player C: Are you a writer?
> Player A: No, I am not Geoffrey Chaucer.
> Player B: Are you a Dickens character?
> Player A: No, I am not Martin Chuzzlewit.

If Player A fails to give a suitable reply because he cannot think of a person with the correct initial in the category mentioned, then the questioner can ask a direct question, to which the answer 'yes' or 'no' must be given. For example, they may ask, 'Are you a fictional character?' 'Are you American?' or 'Are you male?' thus finding out essential information about the chosen character. It follows that Player A must choose a character about whom he or she has some knowledge in order to be able to answer the questions correctly.

The game is won when the guesser correctly identifies the chosen personality, and that player can then choose a character for the next round.

The Minister's Cat

This is an alphabet game for any number of players. Those taking part sit or stand round in a circle, and the first player begins describing the minister's cat with the letter A. He or she might say, for example, 'The minister's cat is an adorable cat and its name is Angela.' The next player has to think of an adjective that could describe the cat and a name for it, also beginning with A. He or she might say, 'The minister's cat is an angry cat and its name is Alphonse.' Play continues in this way until it comes round to the player who started this first round. The letter then changes to B, and everyone has to think of an adjective describing the cat and a name for it beginning with B.

If anyone gets stuck, or repeats something another player has said then he or she is out of the game. The winner (or winners) are those who manage to stay in the game. It is as well to decide beforehand to omit letters like X and Z.

Poison Letters

Any number of players can play this game, but there should be four or more for it to work well. One person is chosen to lead the game, and the players have to answer questions put to them by the leader, avoiding words that contain the 'poison letter'.

For example, if the poison letter is B, the leader would say: 'The Great Panjandrum does not like the letter B. Where can he go for his holidays?'

Players then take it in turns to give an answer. None of the answers must contain the letter B. They might say, 'Penzance', or 'Skye', but if someone says 'Scarborough' then they are out.

In the next round a different letter and a different subject are chosen, and the game continues until only one person is left in the game. He or she is the winner.

Donkey

This is a word game for any number of players. The only equipment you might need is a dictionary.

The object of the game is to be the last player to become a DONKEY, and the way to do that is to avoid being the player who completes the spelling of a word in the game.

One player starts by saying a letter. Let us suppose it is P. The next player then has to follow with a letter which forms part of a real word. So after P, he or she might say A, thinking of PAYMENT, or E, thinking of PEAR. It would be no use, for example, saying J, unless you know a word that begins PJ!

Play continues in this way, with each player contributing a letter and trying to avoid being the one who says the letter which ends the word. If someone does end the word, or if they cannot think of a way of continuing it, they lose a life, and are awarded the letter D. If this happens twice, they get DO, three times

DON, etc., until after six mishaps they become a DONKEY and have to drop out of the game.

If one player suspects that another does not have a real word in mind when adding a letter, but is doing so simply to avoid ending the word, he can challenge that player, who then has to spell out his or her word. (This is where a dictionary comes in useful.) If the challenged player did not have a word in mind, or if he or she was trying to spell it incorrectly, then he or she loses a life, but if there was a proper word in mind, the challenger loses a life. For example, if play had reached P A R A, and someone added an M, it might be challenged by a player who could only think of ending the word with CHUTE to make PARACHUTE. But the challenged player could then say PARAMOUNT, or PARAMETER, in which case the challenger would lose a life.

The last player to become a DONKEY and drop out of the game, wins, and he or she then starts the next game by choosing a letter.

What's Wrong?

The intrepid explorer thinks he's found an ancient Egyptian tomb, but there are a number of very odd things around! How many can you spot?

Wool Gathering

Who will reach the sheep first, the wolf or the shepherd?

Word Games II

All Ways

This pencil and paper word game can be played by a single player or a group. This is what you have to do.

Think of a word — any word will do — and write in the middle of a sheet of paper. Now give yourself, or the group of players, each of whom thinks of their own word, five minutes to add as many words as possible, interlocking them as in a crossword puzzle. All the new words must be in some way related to the original word.

For example, suppose the starting word were PHOTOGRAPH. Here is a grid that could be made from it.

```
e                     c
n               f  l  a  s  h
l  e  n  s            m
a        n      n     e
r        a  f   e     r     s
g        P  H  O  T  O  G  R  A  P  H
e        c      a           o
m        u      t           t
e        s   f  i  l  m
n               v     p        p
t            e  x  p  o  s  u  r  e
                      s        i
             s  l  i  d  e     n
                               t
```

If played as a competitive game, the winner is the person who gets the greatest number of words in his or her grid.

One Hundred Words

This game, which sounds so easy, is in fact quite a difficult task. The idea is to write one hundred words that make sense and not repeat a single word once. People can either try and produce their own effort, or they can work together in teams, but either way there should be an agreed time limit, say fifteen minutes, or the game could continue indefinitely. Here's one example of what can be written.

Let's go! The challenge is to write a composition without using any word more than once. Do you think it can be done? If not, give one reason for doing this. While we are sitting here in the English class at Brownstone Hills Secondary School, Lakeside Avenue, Little Biggington, all of us figure out something which makes sense. Mrs Carruthers helps her pupils because another teacher said they couldn't accomplish such tasks. Nobody has any fresh ideas right now. Goal — 100! How far did students get? Eighty-five done already, fifteen left. 'Pretty soon none!' says Mary Davies. Ben Shepherd and Lisa Anderson agree. So there!

Have a go. It isn't easy, but it is fun, and there is a great sense of achievement when you have done it.

Stairway

This is another pencil and paper word game that can be played by any number of people. One player calls out a letter of the alphabet and the players are then given either five or ten minutes in which to form a 'stairway' of words beginning with that letter. The stairway starts with a two-letter word, and then progresses to a three-letter word, a four-letter word, a five-letter word, and so on. The player who forms the longest stairway in a given time wins.

Here is an example of a stairway for the the letter T.

```
T
T O
T O P
T R A M
T R A I N
T R I C K Y
T R A P E Z E
T E A S P O O N
T H E S A U R U S
T R I A N G U L A R
T E R M I N A T I O N
T O G E T H E R N E S S
```

Worldly Wealth

For these puzzles you will need twelve coins of any denomination.

Twelve Square

Arrange twelve coins in a square like this, with four coins along each side of the square.

Now use the same twelve coins to form another square, with five coins along each side. It is possible!

Ten Triangle

Arrange ten coins in a triangle like this.

By moving three of the coins only, construct a triangle that is pointing downwards instead of upwards.

Heads and Tails — 1

Arrange six coins in a row like this, three with their heads uppermost and three with their tails uppermost.

In three moves, each move consisting of turning over two adjacent coins, arrange them so that the heads and tails are alternating like this.

Heads and Tails — 2

Go back to the position for the previous puzzle, with six coins arranged three head uppermost and three tails uppermost.

In three moves, this time consisting of moving two adjacent coins to a new position, re-arrange them so that they end up with heads and tails alternating, like this. There should not be large gaps between the coins.

207

Coin Cross

Arrange six coins in the form of a cross, like this.

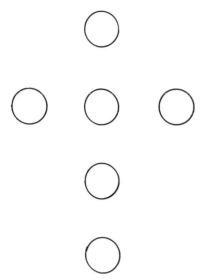

By moving just one of the coins, form two rows with four coins in each row.

Nine Coins

Now take nine coins and arrange them so that you have ten rows with three coins in each row. Stop and think about this one. The answer is very simple, but you may not realize it.

Three Lines

Arrange twelve coins in three straight lines, with an odd number of coins in each line.

Worldly Wisdom

It's Proverbial

If you can find the missing letters in these sentences you will discover a fount of wisdom, for they are all old English proverbs.

1. M I S S I S S G O O D S M I L E
2. O O K B E F O R E Y O U E A P
3. A S T T C H N T M E S A V E S N N E
4. M N Y H N D S M K E L I G H T W O R K
5. T M A N Y C K S S P I L T H E B R T H
6. N E V E R L K A G I F T H R S E I N T H E M U T H
7. A R O L L I N G T O N E G A T H E R N O M O
8. T H A R L Y B I R D C A T C H S T H W O R M
9. A B I R D I N H E H A N D I S W O R H W O I N H E B U S H
10. R L T B D R L T R S M K S M N H L T H W L T H N D W S

Where In the World?

Link each of these wordly features with its number on the map.

Equator   River Mississippi   Cairo   New York
Tropic of Cancer   Mount Everest   Calcutta   Peking
Tropic of Capricorn   Dead Sea   Hong Kong   Rio de Janeiro
International Dateline Falkland Islands   Melbourne   Sydney
River Nile   Buenos Aires   Moscow   Tokyo

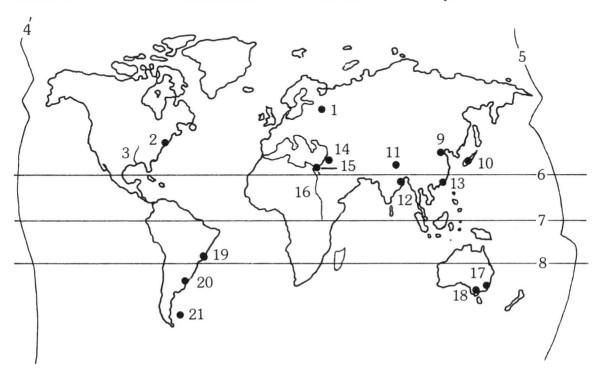

X Marks the Spot

Pudsey Pete, the pirate with the parrot, has found a map of an island where treasure is supposed to be hidden, but unfortunately X does not mark the spot! He has some clues to its whereabouts, however. Given the clues, can you find the treasure?

The map references refer to points where two lines cross.

Clues

The treasure is not hidden at C3, nor at any other place like it.

Don't go fishing at G4 — all you'll find there are fish.

The treasure is not hidden in any square of the map that includes a piece of coastline.

F3 may look promising, but it's a red herring.

The treasure isn't hidden at B3, nor at any other place like it.

You don't have to move any rocks to find the treasure, nor climb a mountain, nor go down a pit.

Beer may once have been kept in here, but there's no treasure here now.

The treasure is not at B2, D3, F5, F6 or H3.

Have you worked out where it is? There is one thing on the island that Pudsey Pete will need to claim the treasure. What is it, and where is it?

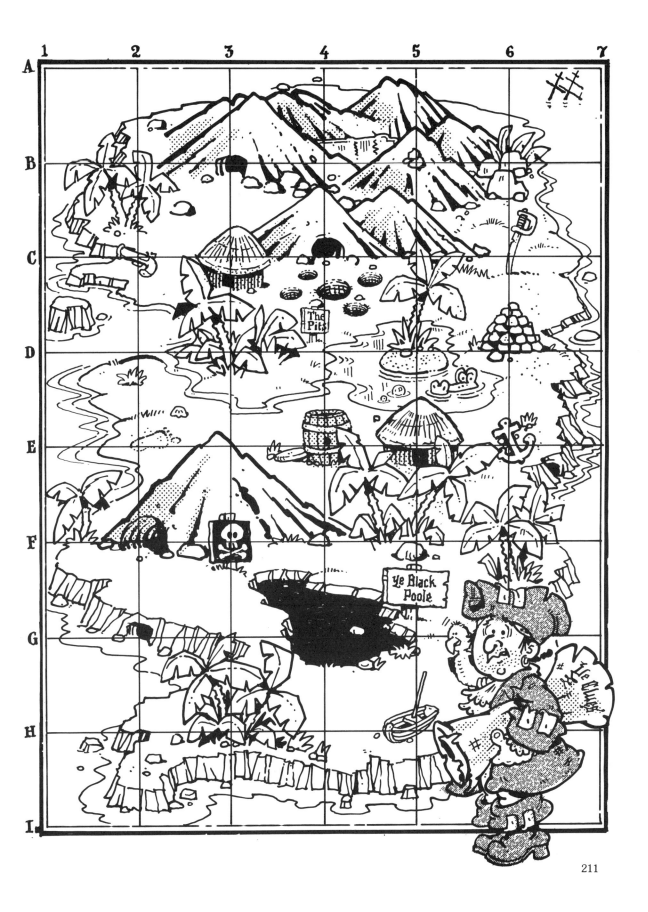

211

Xword Xtra

When you have solved all the clues in this puzzle, you will see that abbreviated forms of the days of the week are spelt out in the shaded squares.

Across
1. Miscellaneous items (8).
5. Take part in a protest march (11).
6. The opposite of 'vice' (6).
9. A root vegetable (5).
12. Round Table sovereign (4, 6).
15. A continent (6).
16. Shiny material (5).

Down
1. Perspire (5).
2. Rope used on gallows (5).
3. Being pulled from behind (2, 3).
4. Rise to one's feet (5).
7. One of the Balearic islands (5).
8. A girl's name (3).
9. An area of London's West End (4).
10. Titled men (5).
11. T. S. ———, a famous poet (5).
13. Young female person (4).
14. Wealthy (4).

Xtravaganza!

There are thirty-four words listed in this word-search puzzle and they all contain the letter X. They may be read across, down or diagonally, either forwards or backwards, but they are always in straight lines. See if you can find them all.

ANNEXE	COMPLEX	IBEX	ORYX	SEX
APEX	EQUINOX	ILEX	PARADOX	SPHINX
APPENDIX	EXTRA	INDEX	PHALANX	SUFFIX
BORAX	FLAX	LARYNX	PHARYNX	STYX
BOX	FLEX	LATEX	PHOENIX	WAX
CLIMAX	FOX	LYNX	PHLOX	XMAS
COAX	HOAX	ONYX	PREFIX	

```
L  X  N  Y  L                      X  B  I  B  X
A  E  X  E  L  I                 I  O  N  Q  M  N
T  B  J  S  T  Y  X            F  R  D  P  A  J  H
E  I  S  P  H  I  N  X      E  A  E  Z  S  F  T  H
X  E  Q  U  I  N  O  X  R  X  X  I  N  E  O  H  P
X  D  V  K  G  Y  P  A  N  N  E  X  E  X  X
   M  W  C  N  L  B  R  V  A  I  X  W  B
      N  O  O  S  W  S  R  D  D  E  X
         M  V  A  J  T  N  M  X  P
            T  P  X  X  X  E  P  X  A  K
            K  H  L  L  E  P  N  C  X  A  K  X
         W  L  N  E  X  P  C  S  Y  X  N  R  Y  E  Q
      X  O  A  K  X  A  L  X  A  U  R  B  A  A  X  L  Y
      X  D  R  V  W  I  L  F      R  F  A  X  L  D  X  F
      O  R  Y  X  M  D  L         T  F  H  X  A  O  H
      B  W  N  A  V  A            X  I  P  V  H  X
      X  X  X  Y  X               E  X  E  S  P
```

Xperts!

Each of these pictures illustrates one of the words below. Do you know which 'ologist' is which?

campanologist
conchologist
entomologist
horologist
odontologist
trichologist

X Certificates

An X certificate used to be awarded to films not suitable for children under eighteen, but the ones in this picture are much more fun, being found in all kinds of unlikely places. How many are there altogether?

Xcrutiating!

Brain teasers to really test your wits.

Old and Young

A man weighed down with years married a young woman. Their combined ages came to 100 years. The man's age, multiplied by 4 and divided by 9, equalled the woman's age. How old were the husband and wife?

Dividing 100

Divide 100 into two parts so that a quarter of one part exceeds a third of the other part by 11.

Dotty

Connect the following nine dots with the smallest number of connected straight lines.

Cider Daze

Gavin Guzzle, a West Country farmer, can drink a barrel of cider in twenty days, but if his wife also drinks some, they finish the barrel in fourteen days. How long would it take Mrs Guzzle to drink the cider on her own?

Smallest Box

There are five boxes of sweets in a shop. Four of the boxes contain 84 sweets between them, but the fifth box contains four sweets fewer than the average of the five boxes. How many sweets are there in the fifth box?

Paintings Puzzle

When Kevin K. Kidlington, a rich art collector, died, he left seventeen paintings to his three children. Half of his paintings he left to Kathleen, his eldest daughter. A third of his paintings he left to Kelvin, his son, and a ninth of his paintings he left to Katie, his youngest daughter.

The three Kidlington heirs had difficulty in making the division, so they borrowed a painting from their rich neighbour, to make eighteen paintings in all. Kathleen took half, or nine; Kelvin took a third, or six; and Katie took a ninth, or two. When they had done this they discovered that they had seventeen paintings between them, so they returned the borrowed painting to the neighbour.

Can you explain what happened?

Longest River

How many times does the letter S occur in the name of the longest river in the world?

Pattern Puzzle

The patterns in the top four squares have something in common. Which of the patterns in the lower eight squares belongs to the top four set?

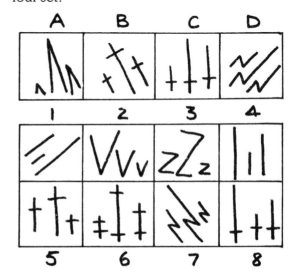

Yes or No?

You have a fifty per cent chance of being right in your answers to these questions, as they can either be answered with a 'yes' or a 'no'.

1. Did Emily Brontë write *Jane Eyre*?
2. Is a viola a flower?
3. Did Schubert write the 'Unfinished Symphony'?
4. Is a metric tonne approximately the same weight as an imperial ton?
5. Is Hamilton the capital of Bermuda?
6. Is an adze used by a bricklayer?
7. Was the Spanish Civil War fought before the First World War?
8. Did Edmund Hillary climb Everest?
9. Is a russet a kind of apple?
10. Did Ali Baba have fifty thieves?

11. Was the French King Louis XIV known as the Sun King?
12. Is a *nom de plume* something to eat?
13. Is Arabic read from right to left?
14. Is a Lamborghini an Italian hat?
15. Is myxomatosis a disease of rabbits?
16. Was the Pharos at Alexandria the ruler of the city?
17. Are cirrus and cumulus types of cloud?
18. Did Jerome K. Jerome write *Three Men in a Boat*?
19. Is the oesophagus a bone in the foot?
20. Are oranges full of vitamin C?

Yellow, Green, Blue

Yellow, green and blue are three of the colours of the rainbow. Do you know what the others are? The answers to the acrostic on this page are all colours, and if you solve all the across clues you will discover another colour in the arrowed column reading down.

1. Yellowish, and something we eat.
2. The colour of sunshine and buttercups.
3. Purplish, and a semi-precious stone.
4. Greeny-blue, and another semi-precious stone.
5. A deep red colour.
6. Another deep red colour.
7. Pale mauve, and a flower.
8. Deep blue, like a cloudless summer sky.
9. Purply-mauve, and another flower.
10. Midnight blue.
11. Deep red, and a fruit.

Y's Words

The answers to the acrostic on this page all begin with the letter Y. Solve the nine clues, and then discover the hidden word in the arrowed column.

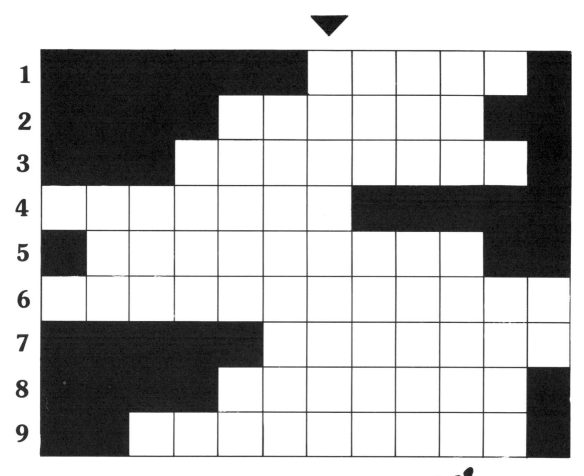

1. Sailing boat.
2. Old-fashioned word for a farmer.
3. A horse or other animal between the ages of one and two.
4. A veil worn by Muslim women.
5. An immature person or animal.
6. A bird with a distinctive song.
7. Jewish language.
8. The total number of yards in something.
9. What today will be tomorrow.

Planet Ywho

Here's a scene from Planet Ywho, full of robots, flying saucers and bug-eyed monsters. Three of the squares in the picture are identical. Can you spot which ones? The squares are identified by the numbers across the top and the letters down the left-hand side, so, for example, the top left-hand square is A1.

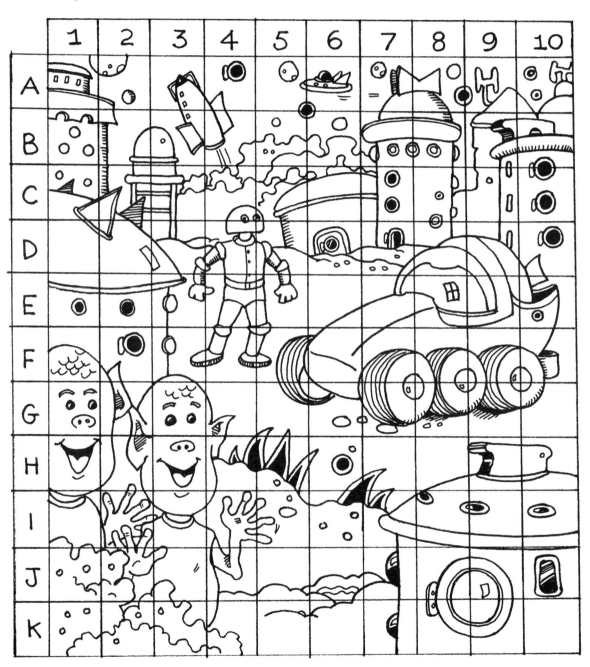

Crammed inside one of the buildings on Planet Ywho, the robots and bug-eyed monsters are having a get-together. How many robots and how many bug-eyed monsters are there in the picture?

Y, OY?

If you can read this heading then you will be able to read the messages spelt out in pictures and letters below. What, you can't read the heading? It says why, oh why, of course!

Zoo Time

Zoo Quiz

Test your knowledge of the animal world with these twenty questions.

1. Pomeranian, weimaraner, schnauzer — what kind of animals are these?
2. What is a Suffolk Punch?
3. Which animals came from the Channel Islands?
4. What is an African Grey?
5. Puma, hyena, ocelot — which is the odd man out?
6. Which bird lays its eggs in other birds' nests?
7. Gorillas are vegetarian — true or false?

8. What kind of sea creature is born in the Sargasso Sea and travels to Europe to mature?
9. Are whales warm-blooded?
10. What kind of animals are associated with Gibraltar?

11. What kind of animal is nicknamed Reynard?
12. What lizard is supposed, in legend, to live in fire?

13. Does a dromedary have two humps?
14. What are peacocks, brimstones and fritillaries?
15. How fast can a racehorse travel over a short distance — 20 mph (32 km/h), 30 mph (48 km/h) or 40 mph (64 km/h)?
16. Cats can see in total darkness — true or false?
17. What is the smallest British bird?
18. What kind of creature is a Rhode Island Red?
19. What is an amphibian?
20. What are sika, fallow, roe and red?

Zoo Words

What do these animal adjectives mean?

1. Catty.
2. Bird-brained.
3. Eagle-eyed.
4. Elephantine.
5. Ratty.
6. Shrewish.
7. Crabby.
8. Mousy.
9. Bovine.
10. Mulish.
11. Cocky.
12. Batty.
13. Sheepish.
14. Dogged.
15. Sluggish.
16. Waspish.

Animal Homes

Each of the animals and birds listed below lives in one of the territories pictured. Which creatures live where?

Mountains

Woodland

Pond

Grassland

River

Badger, bass, beaver, carp, deer, eagle, frog, goat, hare, kingfisher, horse, newt, otter, rabbit, rook, sandpiper, seagull, seal, skylark, squirrel, toad, trout, vole, water snail, wolf, woodpecker.

Zany Zoo Games

Games of all kinds with animal connections.

Beetle

This is a pencil and paper game for two to six players. It requires a die and something to shake it in.

The object of the game is to be the first player to draw a beetle, but the beetle cannot be drawn until the correct numbers have been thrown on the die. The beetle has twelve parts: a head, a body, two eyes, two feelers and six legs, and looks something like this:

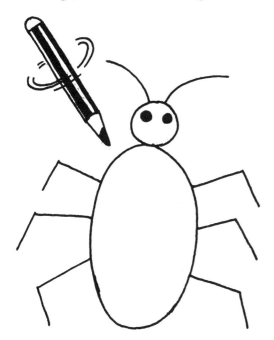

The score for the body has to be thrown before the drawing of the beetle can start, and the score for the head has to be thrown and the head drawn before the feelers and eyes are added. The scores required for drawing the different parts are as follows:

6 for the body
5 for the head
4 for each leg
3 for each eye
2 for each feeler

The winner is the first player to complete his or her beetle.

Fox and Geese

This is a board game for two players, which needs a board like that shown below, which can be drawn on a sheet of paper, thirteen black counters and one white counter (these could be pennies and one 5p piece).

Play starts with the counters positioned as shown in the drawing. The white counter is the fox, and the black counters are the geese. The fox moves first, then the player with the geese moves one of his or her counters, and play continues like this throughout the game. The fox's object is to capture enough geese to prevent them from trapping him, and the geese's ojective is to trap the fox so he cannot move. If the geese player does this they win the game.

Both the fox and the geese can move along any of the lines to a neighbouring vacant point. The fox can capture geese by jumping over them to a vacant point beyond, but the geese cannot jump over the fox, nor can they jump over each other.

If the geese crowd the fox into a corner he cannot move, so they win. But if the fox captures enough geese to prevent them from doing this he wins the game.

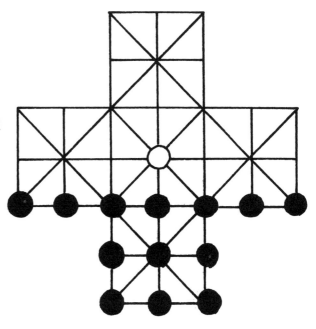

Crab Scuttle Relay

Any even number of players can take part in this team game. They need a course along which to race, which can either be indoors or outdoors.

The players line up at one end of the play area, and on the word 'Go!' the first player of each team runs to the finishing line and back again. He then bends over, puts his hand through his legs, and grabs the hand of the player behind. The two of them then race down to the finishing line and back again in this position — hence the name of the race. When they return to the team, the second player bends down and with his hand through his legs grasps the hand of the third player, and they scuttle down the course and back again. The race proceeds until the whole team has scuttled to the finishing line and back to the start, and the first team to do so wins.

The Dog and the Cat

This is a hilarious game for any number of players. It requires two small objects to represent the 'dog' and the 'cat', such as an eraser and a pencil sharpener.

The players sit in a circle, and one is chosen as the leader. He or she is given the two objects which represent the dog and the cat. The game starts by the leader passing the 'dog' to the player on their left and saying, 'Here is the dog.' The player receiving the object has to ask, 'The what?' And the leader has to reply, 'The dog.' The second player then passes the 'dog' to the player on their left, with the same words, 'Here is the dog,' to which the player again asks, 'The what?' but the second player does not answer, but passes the question back to the leader, who must answer, 'The dog.'

Play continues in this way, with all the players using the same words, and the question 'The what?' always being passed back down the line to the leader. But as soon as the leader has passed the dog, he or she passes the cat to the player on the right, with the same format of words repeated, 'Here is the cat', and when the question 'The what?' is asked, the leader has to answer, 'The cat.'

After a few minutes total chaos ensues, with everyone getting utterly confused about which object is which, and a good deal of fun is had by all. When the objects finally get back round the circle to the leader again, it is best to change the leader to let someone else have a go.

A to Z

All but one of the answers in this crossword begins with a different letter of the alphabet.

Across

1. A climbing evergreen plant; also a girl's name (3).
4. A percussion instrument (9).
9. A game played with clubs and a ball (4).
10. A long, sharp tooth (4).
11. A place where wild animals are kept and displayed (3).
14. The region around the North Pole (6).
17. The result of tying two bits of string together (4).
19. A large feather, formerly used as a pen (5).
21. You and me (2).
22. Seven days (4).
25. A machine which can act like a man (5).
26. A long-haired Tibetan ox (3).

Down

2. A vehicle for carrying goods (3).
3. Belonging to me (4).
5. Something that measures a great distance (4).
6. The opposite of 'off' (2).
7. Hard work and trying hard (6).
8. Run at a slow trot (3).
12. The covering of a tree (4).
13. Someone who studies a lot (7).
15. A ball game played with mallets (7).
18. An elephant has two of them (4).
20. Someone who owns something (5).
23. Something done by the dutiful (4).
24. A bird of prey (4).

Zap, Pow, Twaaang!

The captions to these silly sounds don't match the pictures. Can you put them in the correct places?

Zzzzzzzzzzzzzzz!

All the words in this word-search puzzle contain at least one Z. The words may be read across, down or diagonally, either forwards or backwards, but always in straight lines. They are all listed below. How many can you find?

AMAZON	**MUZZLE**	**ZEST**
AZTEC	**TOPAZ**	**ZIGZAG**
AZURE	**WHIZZ**	**ZINC**
BAZAAR	**ZANY**	**ZIP**
BUZZ	**ZEAL**	**ZIRCONIUM**
CZECH	**ZEBRA**	**ZODIAC**
FIZZ	**ZENITH**	**ZOMBIE**
FUZZ	**ZERO**	**ZONE**

```
Z O O C O O Z W F A H T I N E Z
O O N R O O Z I H Z Z O Z O O Z
O I O O E O Z I O I O T O I O O
Z Z H C E Z C O G Z Z O E D P Z
            Z E Z I C O
            Z I A A O O
          L B M C G
          F M U Z O
        E O I O O
      A L Z N O Z
    T Z M O Z O
  O Z O C A X
Z U O R P Z Z T Y N A Z E L Z F
M Z I O O A O O S O O Z A N O U
A Z U R E Z Z O N E O E Z O O Z
B A Z A A R B U Z Z Z A R B E Z
```

Zebra Zig-zag

The last puzzle in the book is this zany zebra maze. Find your way round the stripes, going in at the mane and out at the back leg.

Answers

A

Amazing 9

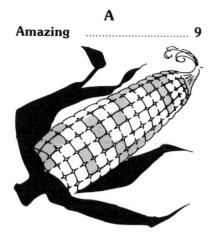

America Ahoy! 10
The United States

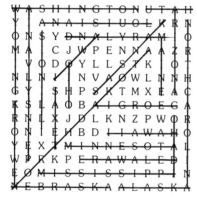

American English
1. Bathtub.
2. Cookie.
3. Cotton candy.
4. Hood.
5. French fries.
6. Crib.
7. Potato chips.
8. Divided highway.
9. Carnival.
10. Bobby pin.
11. Vacation.
12. Popsicle.
13. Truck.
14. Zero.
15. Faucet.
16. Subway.
17. Traffic circle.
18. Jump rope.
19. Undershirt.
20. Closet.

American American
1. The Colorado.
2. Los Angeles.
3. Superior, Michigan, Huron, Erie and Ontario.
4. Bald eagle.
5. The Appalachians.
6. Ten.
7. Baseball.
8. In New York Harbour.
9. At a fortress near San Antonio in Texas, in 1836.
10. The fourth Thursday in November.

Person to Person
1. George Washington.
2. Jane Fonda.
3. Wild Bill Hickok.
4. Marilyn Monroe.
5. Abraham Lincoln.
6. Woody Allen.
7. Henry Ford.
8. Nancy Reagan.

City States
1. Alabama.
2. Massachusetts.
3. Wyoming.
4. Illinois.
5. New Mexico.
6. Tennessee.
7. Pennsylvania.
8. Utah.
9. Washington.
10. Florida.

Flying the Flag
Flag no. 5 is the correct one.

Yankee Doodles
1. Hollywood.
2. Times Square.
3. Stars and stripes.
4. Son of a gun.
5. High school.
6. Pool table.
7. Washington.
8. The White House.
9. Cowboy.
10. Basketball.

B

Baffling Brainteasers 15
On the Buses
Husband and wife.

Day by Daze
Sunday.

Courtship Conundrum
Magnolia with Maurice (the lorry driver).
Monica with Melvin (the doctor).
Matilda with Marmaduke (the accountant).

Housey Housey
Anna £20,000, Barbara £30,000, Clara £10,000.

Broad Acres
Augustus 179,750 acres, Broderick 215,700 acres, Cuthbert 251,650 acres.

Age of Discretion
Susan Ann is ten and her mother is forty.

Shopping Spree
£100.

Postal Puzzle
Five at 2p, fifty at 1p, eight at 5p, making a total of 63 stamps.

Pinta Puzzle
Fill the three-pint jug and empty it into the five-pint jug. Fill the three-pint jug again, empty as much as you can into the five-pint jug, and you are left with one pint in the three-pint jug.

Office Task
Day 1	8 files
Day 2	14 files
Day 3	20 files
Day 4	26 files
Day 5	32 files

Typing Pool
Anna has saved £400, Belinda £100, Clara £15, Doreen £21, Ethel £30, Freda £18, Gloria £300, Harriet £17, Isobel £15, Jenny £150, Kerry £75.

C

Calculator Games 20
Crazy Calculations
The answers are:

        11
       111
      1111
     11111
    111111
   1111111
  11111111
 111111111

Crossword Corner 24

Beginners' Luck

Animal Magic

T-Time

Oooooooo!

Seek and Find

Good Luck!

Cryptic Crossword

Against the Clock

Blankety Blank

Contrariwise

Y	D	E	E	N		S	R	E	D	N	I	H
A		S		E		T		S		I		T
L	A	R	E	T	I	L		N	I	A	L	P
P		E		H		U		E		L		E
S	E	V	I	G		D	E	T	U	L	I	D
I		I		I		A				I		
D	E	Y	A	L	P		E	D	I	V	I	D
		L		T		E				E		E
S	S	E	N	L	L	I		T	E	E	W	S
D		S		E		D		B		D		U
R	A	L	O	P		E	R	U	L	I	A	F
O		A		E		R		O		R		E
L	U	F	E	R	A	C		D	I	P	A	R

Catherine Wheel

M	O	D	E	S	T	R	O	Y	E	R	M	I
S	H	A	N	D	I	C	A	P	A	B	L	N
I	E	G	O	N	E	R	O	U	S	U	E	E
E	R	B	A	N	E	C	T	A	R	R	V	P
G	O	R	I	T	E	M	P	E	T	P	E	T
U	H	U	D	N	D	I	G	S	I	E	R	U
L	P	O	U	I	T	H	O	T	S	R	E	N
E	A	V	R	X	A	I	L	I	A	M	T	E
D	M	A	E	O	T	T	E	L	N	A	R	V
U	E	E	G	A	N	O	R	I	D	F	I	E
T	S	D	N	E	P	I	T	S	O	R	E	R
I	N	E	M	M	I	T	A	B	R	E	V	T
T	L	A	I	T	N	E	S	S	E	L	E	H

D

Dominoes 37
Spots Before the Eyes

1.

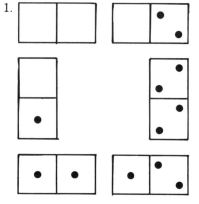

2.

3.

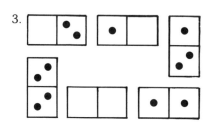

Dotty Doodles 40

1. A giraffe passing a second-storey window.
2. A koala bear climbing the far side of a tree.
3. A Mexican frying an egg (bird's eye view).
4. Two worms making a spectacle of themselves.
5. A mouse hiding behind a stone.
6. A spider doing a handstand.
7. A Mexican cycle race (bird's eye view).
8. A dachshund passing a gap in the fence.
9. A Mexican walking along a railway line (bird's eye view).
10. A sea serpent.

Dotty Dots 41

It's a girl wearing a spotted dress, spotted shoes and spotted hair-ribbons.

Dolls' House 42

There are 21 dolls hidden in the picture.

Dog House 43

There are twelve dogs in the picture.

E
Elementary, My Dear Watson 44
Sherlock Holmes Quiz

1. Sir Arthur Conan Doyle.
2. In London, at 221B Baker Street.
3. Dr Watson.
4. Mrs Hudson.
5. The violin.
6. In a Turkish slipper.
7. *A Study in Scarlet.*
8. 1887.
9. Professor Moriarty.
10. At the Reichenbach Falls.

Find Holmes's Hat and Pipe

The hat is upside down on the cupboard in the window alcove; the pipe is disguised as a handle on the plant holder in the left foreground of the picture.

Crime at Cinderthorpe Hall

Grimsditch the gardener.

Find the Dalrymple Diamonds

Under the rockery in square A3.

Evidence Enough 48
The Case of the Missing First Edition

Miss Prim stole it. One of her hair pins is in the case.

The Case of the Matron's Cheque Book

The man in the wheelchair and the man with his arms in plaster did it together. The man with plaster on his arms walked up the steps to Matron's office and stole her handbag, which he could just pick up. He took it to the man in the wheelchair who forged the cheques, then he replaced the handbag in the office. Neither of the other patients, who were confined to bed, could have climbed the steps to the office.

'Eagle-eye' Edwards and Algernon's Alibi 50

Algernon's alibi is full of contradictions.

1. If Agatha is his aunt, he is not her cousin, but her nephew.
2. The River Clyde does not run through London.
3. The M5 is nowhere near London.

4. It can't have been a warm, dry evening if it was raining.
5. If he left London at 5 o'clock he can't have arrived in Sussex at 5.15.
6. If Aunt Agatha lived in a pretty little cottage she can't also have lived in a block of flats.
7. Her name can't have been 'Mrs Adamson' if she never married.
8. There's no such thing as a £25 note.
9. If he arrived at 5.15 the clock can't have said 6.30 (and even if he didn't the times are still contradictory).
10. If Aunt Agatha lived alone her sister Martha can't have been there.
11. If she had to unwrap the clock Algernon couldn't have seen what time it was telling.
12. The clock has turned into a watch.
13. Where did the fifteen dinner guests come from?
14. Toast and marmalade and cornflakes is a funny way to end dinner.
15. If Aunt Agatha never married her husband couldn't have died.
16. If he came down by car why would he want to catch the train back?
17. He arrived back fifteen minutes before he left.
18. Having travelled back by train, he put the car away.
19. By his own admission, his alibi only takes him up to 11.15 or possibly 11.30, whereas it was required until midnight.

F

Fruity Fun 52
Fruit Machine
The fruits stand for the following numbers:
lemon = 1
blackberry = 2
apple = 3
banana = 4
pear = 5
pineapple = 6

Fruit Picking 54
Twenty-nine apples are ready for picking. One ripe apple has fallen off the tree and two have already been picked.

Fruit and Veg 55
Contained in the picture are a pair of spectacles, a belt, a sock, a comb, a glove, a tennis ball, a golf ball, a book, an egg-cup, a pencil, a paintbrush, a Christmas tree decoration, a bow tie, a fish and a button.

G

Globe Trotting 58
Capital Quiz
1. Paris.
2. Canberra.
3. Accra.
4. Bonn.
5. Islamabad.
6. Riyadh.
7. Montevideo.
8. Madrid.
9. Helsinki.
10. Katmandu.

River Ripples
1. Danube.
2. Amazon.
3. St Lawrence.
4. Jordan.
5. Euphrates.
6. Congo.
7. Ganges.
8. Rio Grande.
9. Tiber.
10. Brahmaputra.

Peaks Puzzle
1. Wales.
2. France.
3. South Africa, or Alaska.
4. Nepal.
5. Switzerland.
6. England.
7. Italy.
8. Northern Ireland.
9. Scotland.
10. Morocco.

Island Hopping
1. North Atlantic.
2. English Channel.
3. North Atlantic.
4. South Pacific.
5. Indian Ocean.
6. North Sea.
7. South Atlantic.
8. Mediterranean Sea.
9. Irish Sea.
10. North Atlantic.

National Emblems
1. Russia.
2. England.
3. France.
4. New Zealand.

Map Reading
1. Quarry.
2. Coniferous wood.
3. Lighthouse (in use).
4. Railway cutting.
5. Church or chapel with tower.
6. Church or chapel with spire.

National Flags
1. Canada.
2. Switzerland.
3. France.
4. Norway.

Getting There 60

Going Places 61
1. Along the motorways.
2. By travelling to Greystoke House, then Curlew Castle, then Hill House, then Condor Castle (via Zedford), then returning to Aford via the wildlife park.
3. You could go by train from Zedford to the gardens at Curlew Castle.
4. The church in Zedford.
5.

6.

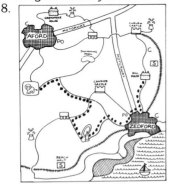

7. Yes, if you don't mind travelling along the ordinary roads as well.

8.

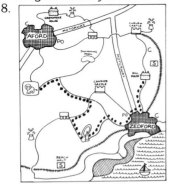

General Knowledge Test 64

Sport Scene
1. 22 yards (20·12 metres).
2. Sheffield Wednesday football team.
3. Six.
4. 26 miles 385 yards (42·195 kilometres).
5. New Zealand rugby team.
6. Tennis.
7. Four.
8. Leeds United.
9. Boxing.
10. A classic flat race for fillies.

Famous Families
1. Wendy, John and Michael.
2. Anne Boleyn.
3. Laszlo and Georg Biro.
4. The Montgolfier brothers.
5. Montague and Capulet.
6. Henry Fonda, Jane Fonda and Peter Fonda.
7. Princess Anne and Mark Phillips.
8. Anne, Charlotte and Emily Brontë.
9. William Pitt, First Earl of Chatham, and William Pitt the Younger (also George and

William Grenville).
10. Richard and David Attenborough.

Animal World
1. Two.
2. They were both originally bred as sheepdogs.
3. Cats.
4. 4 inches (10·6 cm).
5. A giraffe.
6. The badger.
7. A leveret.
8. A squirrel.
9. The hippopotamus.
10. A bat.

Books and Writers
1. Peter Rabbit's.
2. Raymond Briggs.
3. Arthur Ransome.
4. Winnie the Pooh.
5. Sherlock Holmes.
6. Roald Dahl.
7. The Famous Five, in the Enid Blyton books.
8. Richmal Crompton.
9. 007.
10. The Mr Men characters.

Where in the World?
1. The Indian Ocean.
2. Italy.
3. In Antarctica.
4. North and South Island, New Zealand.
5. Afghanistan and Pakistan.
6. Mali.
7. Romania.
8. Canada and Greenland.
9. France.
10. Egypt.

Trivia Challenge
1. End of restriction.
2. The monetary unit of Poland.
3. Queen Guinevere.
4. An entertainment at night involving floodlights and recorded sound, usually recounting events about a building's history.
5. David Penhaligon.
6. An area of central Scotland.
7. Pablo (Ruiz y).
8. Birmingham and Exeter.
9. A famous art gallery in Paris.
10. Florence Nightingale.

H
Holiday Time 66
How Far?
1. 340 km/210 miles.
2. 2350 km/1460 miles.
3. 950 km/590 miles.
4. 400 km/250 miles.
5. 1325 km/823 miles.
6. 440 km/275 miles.
7. 450 km/280 miles.
8. 1535 km/954 miles.
9. 1797 km/1116 miles.
10. 64 km/40 miles.

Airport Codes
Amsterdam — AMS
Athens — ATH
Cairo — CAI
Cape Town — CPT
Delhi — DEL
Geneva — GVA
Hong Kong — HKG
London (Heathrow) — LHR
San Francisco — SFO.
Venice — VCE

Landmarks
1. New York — it's the Statue of Liberty.
2. Sydney — it's Sydney Opera House.
3. Paris — it's the Arc de Triomphe.

Foreign Phrases
1. Good morning, good afternoon, good day (Italian).
2. Thank you, madam (French).
3. Goodbye (Spanish).
4. Good evening (German).

Shoe Shine
1. 28.
2. 38.
3. 40.

Foreign Foods
France
champignons — mushrooms
épinard — spinach
homard — lobster
oeufs — eggs

Germany
brot — bread
sauerkraut — pickled white cabbage
schinken — ham
torten — pastries

Italy
formaggio — cheese
gelato — ice-cream
pesca — peach
pollo — chicken

Spain
fresas — strawberries
oliva — olive
pescado — fish
tortilla — omelette

High Life 68

Hither and Thither 69
Eighteen people are going to Here-Abouts; seven to There-Abouts.

Holiday Crossword 70

(crossword grid with answers: GAP, GEAR, RARE, SHELL, SUDE, SANDCASTLE, SHINA, YARMOUTH, BIRD, PIER, SEAMIST, BEACH, MOTEL, etc.)

Holiday Resorts 71

(word search grid with resorts: BRIDLINGTON, SOUTHEND, KINSALE, GREAT YARMOUTH, ST IVES, MORECAMBE, BRIGHTON, etc.)

Holiday Special 74
1. Copenhagen.
2. Amsterdam.
3. Paris.
4. Lausanne.
5. Vienna.
6. Biarritz.
7. Cannes.
8. Monte Carlo.
9. Venice.
10. Salzburg.
11. Gibraltar.
12. Ibiza.
13. Florence.
14. Rome.
15. Sorrento.
16. Crete.
17. Rhodes.
18. Cyprus.
19. Palermo.
20. Dubrovnik.

Holiday Package 75
The correct order of the pictures is 1, 5, 7, 3, 4, 2, 6, 9, 8.

I

Incalculable 76
Weekends Off
49.

One Number
1.

Driving Test
300 miles.

Soldiers
East.

Vowel-less
Onion.

Potty Problem
27 lbs.

Unlucky Thirteen
R. All the others are the initial letters of the months of the year.

Art Collectors
Three: one Turner, one Constable and one Monet.

What's Next?
65. Each time you double the previous number and subtract 1.

Er, What?
UND ERGRO UND.

I Beg Your Pardon!
A nod is as good as a wink to a blind horse.

Truth Test
Gillie.

Ninety-nine
66.

Party Treats
One bag of chocolates, ten bags of toffees and nine bags of fruit gums.

Car Cleaning
3½ minutes.

Sleepyhead
9.30.

Jane's Jeans
The jeans cost £20.50 and the belt 50p.

Just Supposing

15.

Subtraction

Once. After that you'd be subtracting it from 37, 32, etc.

Number, Please

18.

Leap Year

One hour.

Introducing Cryptarithmetic 78

Roman Riddle

```
  23
  23
  23
 +23
 ___
  92
```

Find Me

```
   5
   5
 + 5
 __
  15
```

Scrabble

```
  7088062
+17531908
_____
 24619970
```

Urgent Plea

```
 9467
+ 1085
_____
 10652
```

Fly For Your Life

```
  598
  507
+8047
____
 9152
```

Seamstress

8 x 4973 = 39784

Adding Up to Sixty

```
   850
   850
+29786
_____
 31486
```

Adding Up to Twelve

```
    106      or       104
  19722             19722
+ 82524           + 82526
_____           _____
 102352            102352
```

1. Charles Babbage — computer.
2. Alexander Graham Bell — telephone.
3. Christopher Cockerell — hovercraft.
4. Rudolf Diesel — diesel engine.
5. Thomas Edison — electric light.
6. Michael Faraday — dynamo.
7. Alexander Fleming — penicillin.
8. Benjamin Franklin — lightning conductor.
9. King Camp Gillette — safety razor.
10. Johann Gutenberg — printing.
11. Joseph Lister — antiseptics.
12. Guglielmo Marconi — radio telegraphy.
13. Joseph and Etienne Montgolfier — balloon.
14. Joseph and Claude Niepce — camera.
15. Jacob Schick — electric razor.
16. Percy Shaw — 'cats'-eyes'.
17. Alessandro Volta — battery.
18. Frank Whittle — jet engine.
19. Lewis Edison Waterman — fountain pen.
20. Wilbur and Orville Wright — aeroplane.

1. Sicily.
2. Madagascar.
3. Isle of Wight.
4. Iceland.
5. Cyprus.
6. South Island, New Zealand.
7. Ireland.
8. Corsica.
9. Shetland.
10. The Isle of Skye.
11. Japan.
12. Australia.

J

Carol Singing

All have one mistake in them.
1. The second line should begin, 'The **little** Lord Jesus'.
2. The second line should begin, '**Joyful**'.
3. The fourth line should read, 'The holly **bears** the crown'.
4. The first line should end, '**gentlemen**'.
5. The last line should begin, '**God** and'.

6. The last line should begin, 'That **glorious** song'.

True or False?

1. True.
2. False, it is 6 December.
3. True.
4. True.
5. False, it is considered to be lucky.
6. True.
7. False, it is by Charles Dickens.
8. True.
9. False, it is forbidden to be hung in churches because of its former pagan associations.
10. False, they should be taken down by 6 January.

Christmas Hits

'Blue Christmas' — Elvis Presley and Shakin' Stevens (pics. 6 and 9).
'Christmas Alphabet' — Dickie Valentine (pic. 3).
'Little Drummer Boy' — David Bowie and Bing Crosby (pics. 1 and 8).
'Make a Daft Noise for Christmas' — The Goodies (pic. 7).
'Mary's Boy Child' — Harry Belafonte (pic. 2).
'Merry Christmas Everybody' — Slade (pic. 10).
'When a Child is Born' — Johnny Mathis (pic. 4).
'White Christmas' — Bing Crosby (pic. 8).
'Wonderful Christmastime' — Paul McCartney (pic. 5).

January Jaunt 89
Picture 4 contains the snowball from 1, the cat from 2, the dog from 3, the holly from 5 and the cloud (the clown's hair) from 6.

January Brings... 90
Snowstorm
Snowflakes numbers 6 and 19 are identical.

Snowman

Jumpers and Boots 95

K
Kids' Stuff 96
Pocket Money
Sally has spent £1.37, and has 13p left out of her £1.50.
Simon has spent £1.08, and has 42p left out of his £1.50.

Bag of Goodies
There are nine different kinds of sweets in the bag.

Rhyme Time
Sun and FUN, chair and pear, door and core, fly and pie, key and knee, pen and hen, hand and band, bird and WORD, cat and mat, dog and log.

Crossed Wires
Andrew (1) has Walkman C; Ben (2) has Walkman A; and Chrissy (3) has Walkman B.

Trouble Decker

Crazy Maypole
The mistakes are: the sparrow's tail, the fish leaf, the dog's feet, the pig in the kangaroo's pouch, the butterfly's odd wing, the cat's tail, the lack of spokes in one of the bike's wheels, the grapes growing in the tree, the horse's tail, and the rabbit's tail.

L
Ladder Words 103
HEAD, HEAL, TEAL, TELL, TALL, TAIL.
FOUR, FOUL, FOOL, FOOT, FORT, FORE, FIRE, FIVE.
RICH, RICK, ROCK, ROOK, BOOK, BOOR, POOR.

Little and Large 104
Central Circles
Both circles are the same size.

Longer Line
They are both the same length.

Longest Line
They are all the same length.

Matchstick Men
They are all the same height.

Tallest Building
1. The Sears Tower.

Largest Palace
3. Versailles.

Largest Block of Flats
2. In the Barbican area of London.

Smallest House
2. In Wales.

Largest Ship
1. The *Queen Elizabeth*.

Largest Bookshop
2. Foyles in London.

Highest Mountain
2. Ben Nevis.

Shortest River
3. The D River.

Longest-reigning King
3. George III.

Shortest-reigning Monarch
3. Jane.

Largest City
3. Tokyo.

Smallest Stamp
3. The Colombian State of Bolivar.

M
Musical Medley 107
What's in a Name?
They are 5 Star.

It's Instrumental

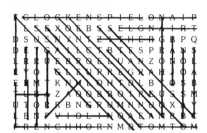

Pop the Question

'Colour By Numbers' — Culture Club
'It's a Miracle' — Culture Club
'Right By Your Side' — Eurythmics
'Touch' — Eurythmics
'An Innocent Man' — Billy Joel
'Wouldn't It Be Good' — Nik Kershaw
'Joanna' — Kool and the Gang
'99 Red Balloons' — Nena
'Keep Moving' — Madness
'The Sun and the Rain' — Madness
'Cafe Bleu' — Style Council
'Into the Gap' — Thompson Twins
'My Guy' — Tracey Ullman
'War' — U2

Groovy!

One groove on each side.

Bits and Pieces

It's Madonna.

Pop Party

Places
1. Chicago.
2. New Orleans.
3. West Virginia.
4. The Rolling Stones.
5. France.
6. Georgia.

Names — 1
1. John Lennon.
2. Cat Stevens.
3. a) Boy George.
   b) Elton John.
   c) Bob Dylan.
   d) Culture Club.
   e) Limahl.
   f) Cliff Richard.

g) Elvis Costello.
h) Shakin' Stevens.

Events
1. Michael Jackson's.
2. Donovan.
3. Bill Haley and the Comets.
4. Amsterdam.
5. Lonnie Donegan's.
6. David Bowie.

Names — 2
1. Howard Jones.
2. Captain Sensible.
3. Alison Moyet.
4. Paul McCartney.
5. Tina Turner.
6. Elton John.
7. Rod Stewart.
8. Diana Ross.

Numbers and Colours
1. Twenty-four.
2. Mick Jagger, in the Rolling Stones's record.
3. Fifty.
4. Eight miles.
5. Elvis Presley.
6. The Beatles.

Names — 3
1. Jude.
2. Rosie.
3. Barbara Ann.
4. Joe DiMaggio.
5. Bob Dylan's.
6. Marie.

Mistakes
1. '**Mull** of Kintyre'.
2. '**Cry** Just a Little Bit'.
3. '**Rat** Rapping'.
4. '**Lust** for Life'.
5. 'Jumping **Jack** Flash'.
6. '**Karma** Chameleon'.
7. 'Ain't No **Mountain** High Enough'.
8. '**Yellow** Submarine'.
9. 'Everything I **Own**'.
10. 'I Wanna **Hold** Your Hand'.

Musical Miscellany 117

Musicals

1. *West Side Story.*
2. *Kiss Me, Kate.*
3. T.S. Eliot's *Old Possum's Book of Practical Cats.*
4. *Cabaret.*
5. *Evita.*

A Night at the Opera

1. It has an all-male cast.
2. *The Mikado.*
3. *The Flying Dutchman.*
4. *Tosca.*
5. *The Marriage of Figaro* was written by Mozart; *The Barber of Seville* was written by Rossini.
6. *Carmen.*
7. True.
8. *La Traviata.*

People and Instruments

1. Andrew Lloyd Webber — composing; Julian Lloyd Webber — playing the cello.
2. Chopin and Liszt.
3. Clarinet; it is a woodwind, the others are brass instruments.
4. Six.
5. a) Guitar and lute.
   b) Cello.
   c) Flute.
   d) Violin.
6. Antonio Vivaldi.
7. Jean Sibelius.
8. J. S. Bach.
9. By blowing it.
10. The violin.
11. All except the cornet and the tuba.
12. Saint-Saëns.

N

Nursery Rhymes 118

Beginnings...

The lines are either written backwards or have been written out without their vowels.
1. Twinkle, twinkle, little star.
2. Jack and Jill went up the hill.
3. Old Mother Hubbard went to the cupboard.
4. Three lttle kittens, they lost their mittens.
5. Little Miss Muffet sat on a tuffet.
6. Mary, Mary, quite contrary.
7. Georgie Porgie, pudding and pie.
8. Little Boy Blue, come blow your horn.
9. Diddle diddle dumpling, my son John.
10. Pussy cat, pussy cat, where have you been?
11. Ride a cock horse to Banbury Cross.
12. Simple Simon met a pieman going to the fair.
13. There was a little girl who had a little curl.

14. The Queen of Hearts, she made some tarts.
15. Sing a song of sixpence.
16. Baa, baa black sheep, have you any wool?
17. Little Bo Peep, she lost her sheep.
18. Hickory, dickory, dock.
19. Wee Willie Winkie runs through the town.
20. Goosey, goosey gander.

...and Endings

1. Hey, diddle, diddle, the cat and the fiddle.
2. Here we go round the mulberry bush.
3. There was an old woman who lived in a shoe.
4. Rub-a-dub-dub, three men in a tub.
5. Pat-a-cake, pat-a-cake, baker's man.
6. I love little pussy.
7. Little Boy Blue, come blow your horn.
8. Mary, Mary, quite contrary.
9. Jack and Jill went up the hill.
10. Ride a cock-horse to Banbury Cross.

Who?

1. Goosey, goosey, gander.
2. Wee Willie Winkie.
3. Little Bo Peep's sheep, in her dream.
4. The queen, in 'Sing a song of sixpence'.
5. Little Polly Flinders.
6. Jack Sprat.
7. The farmers, in 'This is the way the ladies ride'.
8. Simple Simon.
9. Old Mother Hubbard.
10. Little Miss Muffet.

Needle in a Haystack 120

```
L D E N E E D E L N E E N E D
E E N E D L E N E E D E L N E
E E L E N D L E E D E N E E D
D N E L E E N E L E E L E E N
E E L D E E D N L E D E N D E
N L E E D E L E D E E N E L E
E D E N N E E L E D L E N D E
E D E L E E D E E L D E L L
L E N E L D L E N E E L D N E
D E D L N E E E D L E N E E D
E L D E L N E L E N E D E D N
E E D N E D E D E E D E N L E
E L D E E E E L N E E L E D E
E D E L D E N E E D L N E E L
N D E E L E N E N E E L D E E
```

Numbing Number Puzzles 121

The Missing Numbers

1. Nine.
2. Five.
3. Seven.
4. *20,000.*
5. *Three.*
6. *Three.*
7. *Thirty-nine.*
8. Hundred.
9. Sixes and sevens.
10. Two.

Complete the Box

12. The numbers in the central column are made up from the number of 3s contained in the outer column. Thus, in the first line, the first digit of 39 refers to three 3s in 9, the second digit of 39 refers to nine 3s in 27. In the last line, the 4 of 24 indicates four 3s, which are 12.

Eight Eights

```
  888
   88
    8
    8
+   8
 1000
```

Treading the Boards

58.

Spending Power

£1.44.

Three Dozen

Into four 8s. Then 6 + 2 = 8; 10 − 2 = 8; 4 × 2 = 8; 16 ÷ 2 = 8.
6 + 10 + 4 + 16 = 36.

Odd Man Out

1. 54. All the others are multiples of 7.
2. 39. All the others are prime numbers.
3. 35. All the others are numbers of days in the months.
4. 36. All the others are multiples of 13.
5. 7½. All the others refer to the pre-metric measurements of length: 12 ins = 1 ft, 3 ft = 1 yd, 5½ yds = 1 rod, pole or perch, 22 yds = 1 chain, 10 chains = 1 furlong, 8 furlongs = 1 mile.
6. 89. All the others are multiples of 9.
7. 30. All the others refer to the avoirdupois measurements of weight: 16 oz = 1 lb, 14 lb = 1 stone, 2 stones = 1 quarter, 4 quarters = 1 hundredweight, 20 hundredweights = 1 ton.
8. 75. All the others are numbers of pence in sterling coins.

Next, Please

31. There are two series alternating. 7, 9, 13, 21, 37, which adds 2, 4, 8 and 16 to make the series; and 13, 16, 20, 25, 31, which adds 3, 4, 5, and 6.

Trick Question

The trick is to use Roman numerals. Thus XIX, take away I = XX, or 20!

Score a Century

```
   15
   36
   47
+   2
  100
```

Magic Number Square

28	35	12	19	26
34	16	18	25	27
15	17	24	31	33
21	23	30	32	14
22	29	36	13	20

Six has been added to each number in the second example, and each line, column and diagonal now adds up to 120.

Symbolic

The symbols stand for the following numbers:

circle = 1
square = 2
spring = 3
triangle = 4
cross = 5
coil = 6

Figure It Out

$1 + 5 = 6$
$4 + 3 = 7$
$2 + 7 = 9$
$6 + 10 = 16$
$8 + 9 = 17$

Odd Number

12,111. If you got it wrong, add it up as a sum:

```
 11000
  1100
    11
 12111
```

Round Dozen

$11 + {}^{11}\!/_{11} = 12$

Digital Daze

4368.

Two Twos

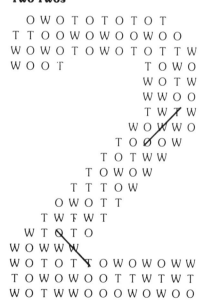

Three Threes

```
      T R E E T H
     T H R R E R T
    R H E E T H R T R E
  H T E E H E R T H E E R
  T H E R T H E E R T H E
                  E R T E
                  T R E E
      R E H T E R E H T
    T R E E E H R E H T
    T H R T E R H E R
    E T H E R E E H T T
      T H T E E R E T H
              T E E T
            H R E E
  T E E T H R E H T H R E
  R T E T H R E T R T T H
    R H E T T R E E T H
      T H E R T E T E
      T E T H R E
```

O

Opposites 126

Sour and sweet, near and far, silence and noise, war and peace, happiness and misery, safe and hazardous, straight and curved, noxious and wholesome, novel and traditional, nadir and zenith, broken and whole, jagged and smooth, famous and unknown, flexible and rigid, body and mind, private and public, vanish and materialize, monotony and variety, reactionary and progressive, prologue and epilogue.

Outsiders 127

1. Glove; all the others are worn on the feet.
2. Giraffe; all the others can be ridden.
3. Tomato, it is a fruit; all the others are vegetables.
4. Honey; all the others are sour.
5. Badger; all the others are domestic animals.
6. Pencil sharpener; all the others are used to write with.

Observation Test 128

Market Stalls

1. 30p per lb.
2. Half price.
3. One.
4. Half-past three.
5. The stall-holder serving the lady.
6. A teddy bear.
7. He is holding his jacket lapels.
8. Bananas.
9. Two.
10. The little boy.

Building Site

1. The chimney is a thermos flask.
2. There is a knot in the scaffolding.
3. There is no cross-piece in the scaffolding at the top on the right.
4. There is a gap in the scaffolding.
5. The scaffolding at the bottom is resting on a bucket.
6. The bricklayer's hod is upside down.
7. He is wearing a woman's apron.
8. He has bare feet.
9. One window is upside down, the sill is at the top.
10. The other bricklayer is laying a loaf of bread.
11. He is using a child's spade.
12. There is a letterbox in the wall.
13. A gardening fork is being used to mix cement.
14. There is a door halfway up the house's wall.
15. Above the door is a tap.

Owl and Ostrich 131

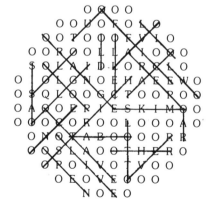

242

Ornithological 132

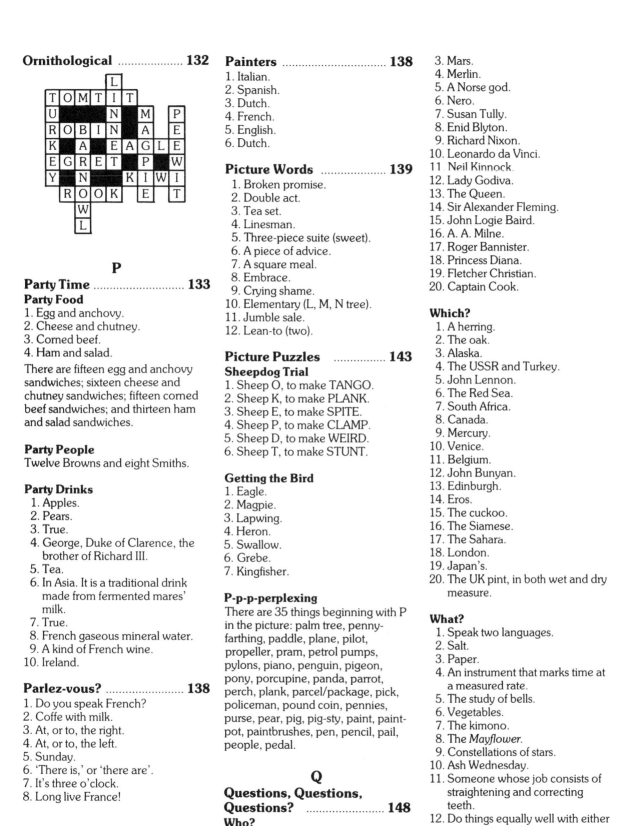

Crossword grid contents:
L
TOMTIT
U N M P
ROBIN A E
K A EAGLE
EGRET P W
Y N KIWI T
ROOK E T
W
L

P

Party Time 133

Party Food
1. Egg and anchovy.
2. Cheese and chutney.
3. Corned beef.
4. Ham and salad.

There are fifteen egg and anchovy sandwiches; sixteen cheese and chutney sandwiches; fifteen corned beef sandwiches; and thirteen ham and salad sandwiches.

Party People
Twelve Browns and eight Smiths.

Party Drinks
1. Apples.
2. Pears.
3. True.
4. George, Duke of Clarence, the brother of Richard III.
5. Tea.
6. In Asia. It is a traditional drink made from fermented mares' milk.
7. True.
8. French gaseous mineral water.
9. A kind of French wine.
10. Ireland.

Parlez-vous? 138
1. Do you speak French?
2. Coffe with milk.
3. At, or to, the right.
4. At, or to, the left.
5. Sunday.
6. 'There is,' or 'there are'.
7. It's three o'clock.
8. Long live France!

Painters 138
1. Italian.
2. Spanish.
3. Dutch.
4. French.
5. English.
6. Dutch.

Picture Words 139
1. Broken promise.
2. Double act.
3. Tea set.
4. Linesman.
5. Three-piece suite (sweet).
6. A piece of advice.
7. A square meal.
8. Embrace.
9. Crying shame.
10. Elementary (L, M, N tree).
11. Jumble sale.
12. Lean-to (two).

Picture Puzzles 143
Sheepdog Trial
1. Sheep O, to make TANGO.
2. Sheep K, to make PLANK.
3. Sheep E, to make SPITE.
4. Sheep P, to make CLAMP.
5. Sheep D, to make WEIRD.
6. Sheep T, to make STUNT.

Getting the Bird
1. Eagle.
2. Magpie.
3. Lapwing.
4. Heron.
5. Swallow.
6. Grebe.
7. Kingfisher.

P-p-p-perplexing
There are 35 things beginning with P in the picture: palm tree, penny-farthing, paddle, plane, pilot, propeller, pram, petrol pumps, pylons, piano, penguin, pigeon, pony, porcupine, panda, parrot, perch, plank, parcel/package, pick, policeman, pound coin, pennies, purse, pear, pig, pig-sty, paint, paint-pot, paintbrushes, pen, pencil, pail, people, pedal.

Q

Questions, Questions, Questions? 148
Who?
1. St Andrew.
2. William Shakespeare.

3. Mars.
4. Merlin.
5. A Norse god.
6. Nero.
7. Susan Tully.
8. Enid Blyton.
9. Richard Nixon.
10. Leonardo da Vinci.
11. Neil Kinnock.
12. Lady Godiva.
13. The Queen.
14. Sir Alexander Fleming.
15. John Logie Baird.
16. A. A. Milne.
17. Roger Bannister.
18. Princess Diana.
19. Fletcher Christian.
20. Captain Cook.

Which?
1. A herring.
2. The oak.
3. Alaska.
4. The USSR and Turkey.
5. John Lennon.
6. The Red Sea.
7. South Africa.
8. Canada.
9. Mercury.
10. Venice.
11. Belgium.
12. John Bunyan.
13. Edinburgh.
14. Eros.
15. The cuckoo.
16. The Siamese.
17. The Sahara.
18. London.
19. Japan's.
20. The UK pint, in both wet and dry measure.

What?
1. Speak two languages.
2. Salt.
3. Paper.
4. An instrument that marks time at a measured rate.
5. The study of bells.
6. Vegetables.
7. The kimono.
8. The *Mayflower*.
9. Constellations of stars.
10. Ash Wednesday.
11. Someone whose job consists of straightening and correcting teeth.
12. Do things equally well with either hand.
13. Wind speed.

14. Distance travelled on foot.
15. Toast and cheese.
16. The ancestral line of an animal.
17. A fruit similar to a raspberry.
18. Pottery.
19. An open-sided gallery on a house.
20. Grass cut and preserved for animal feed.

Where?
1. In Westminster Abbey.
2. In Paris.
3. Oysters.
4. In the Vatican.
5. On your back, it is your shoulder blade.
6. On a flower.
7. In Western Scotland.
8. On the Riviera.
9. In Russia.
10. On the southern tip of Africa.
11. Over a door or window.
12. At a chemist's shop.
13. On a horse's bridle.
14. Off the north-eastern coast of Australia.
15. In Wiltshire.
16. In Ireland.
17. In the Isle of Man.
18. At the entrance to a castle.
19. On an aeroplane.
20. At Aintree, near Liverpool.

How Many?
1. Six.
2. Two.
3. Eleven.
4. Eight.
5. Four.
6. Twenty-four.
7. Five.
8. Ten.
9. 144.
10. Eight.
11. 744.
12. Six.
13. Thirty-two.
14. 1000.
15. Two or four.
16. Twelve.
17. Four.
18. 640.
19. Thirty.
20. Four.

Silly Questions
1. A towel.
2. Your lap.
3. Your breath.
4. A promise.
5. A candle.

Quantity of Quaggas 151
Baby quagga no. 3 is identical to its mother.

R
R.S.V.P. *et al.* 152
English Abbreviations
1. Bachelor of Arts, *or* British Airways.
2. British Broadcasting Corporation.
3. Criminal Investigation Department.
4. Cash on delivery.
5. Football Association.
6. Greenwich Mean Time.
7. Her Majesty's Stationery Office.
8. Imperial Chemical Industries.
9. Lawn Tennis Association.
10. Member of the British Empire.
11. Marylebone Cricket Club.
12. National Society for the Prevention of Cruelty to Children.
13. On Her Majesty's Service.
14. Please turn over.
15. Royal Navy.
16. Royal Society for the Prevention of Cruelty to Animals.
17. Unidentified flying object.
18. Value added tax.
19. Very high frequency.
20. Young Women's Christian Association.

Foreign Abbreviations
1. *Ante meridiem* — before noon.
2. *Exempli gratis* — for example.
3. *Et alii* — and others.
4. *Et cetera* — and the like.
5. *Ibidem* — in the same place.
6. *Id est* — that is.
7. *Nota bene* — mark well.
8. *Post meridiem* — after noon.
9. *Répondez, s'il vous plaît* — please reply.
10. *Videlicet* — namely.

Acronyms
1. Light Amplification by Stimulated Emission of Radiation.
2. National and Local Government Officers' Association.
3. National Aeronautics and Space Administration.
4. North Atlantic Treaty Organization.
5. Oxford Committee for Famine Relief.
6. Quasi Non-Governmental Organization.
7. Quasi-Stellar Object.
8. Radio Detection and Ranging.
9. United Nations Organization.
10. United Nations Educational, Scientific, and Cultural Organization.

Jargon
1. For sale. Semi-detached 3-bedroomed bungalow, with living-room, dining-room, kitchen, bathroom, separate W.C., central heating, good-sized garden, garage. Near schools, station and shops.
2. Country house hotel. Twelve bedrooms, all with hot and cold running water. Six bathrooms, television lounge, good home cooking, fabulous views.
3. Wanted, shorthand typist with speeds of 120/60 words per minute. References required. Hours to suit applicant.

Chemical Symbols
1. Silver.
2. Aluminium.
3. Gold.
4. Carbon.
5. Calcium.
6. Chlorine.
7. Cobalt.
8. Copper.
9. Iron.
10. Hydrogen.
11. Mercury.
12. Iodine.
13. Potassium.
14. Magnesium.
15. Nitrogen.
16. Oxygen.
17. Lead.
18. Sulphur.
19. Tin.
20. Zinc.

Fifty Famous Riddles **153**

Adam
'Madam I'm Adam.'

Angel
'Halo.'

Auctioneer
Lots.

Bed
At night, because two feet are added to it.

Bird
A crane.

Boiled
Iced tea with lemon.

Break
A promise.

Bus
Columbus.

Cars
Where there's a fork in the road.

Clock
The second hand.

Code
S.O.S.

Cows
Because their horns don't work.

Dark
A shadow.

Dimple
A pimple that goes the other way.

Eat
In February, because it's the shortest month.

End
The letter G.

Farmer
A farmer gathers what he sows, a dressmaker sews what she gathers.

Garden
The fence.

Heavy
They are both the same weight.

House
The roof.

I
When you are saying, 'I is the letter that comes after H.'

Instruments
Drums.

Invention
Windows.

Ireland
Cork.

Jam
Because it saw the apple turnover.

Lengthened
A ditch.

London
The letter N.

Man
His barber.

Manicurist
Because she made money hand over fist.

Mayonnaise
Because it is always dressing.

Months
They all do.

Music
A sharp major.

Net
When the water is frozen into ice.

Noah
In the ark hives.

Organist
An organist knows the stops and a cold in the head stops the nose.

P
Because it is near O.

Penny
Because they are both coppers.

Playing Cards
Because they both come in packs.

Run
Water.

S
Because it turns our milk into sour milk.

Secrets
Because corn has ears.

Sheep
There are more white sheep.

Sock
Because you are putting your foot in it.

Tomorrow
Our clothes, when we go to bed.

Trees
Palms.

Vowels
Because all the others are in audible.

Water
Holes.

Westminster Abbey
Because it contains the ashes of the great.

Word
Sixty.

Year
March fourth.

S

Crack a Code
1. Meet Baxter to pick up sausages.
2. Check Cecil's trousers for clues.
3. Follow Fred on trip to Tadworth.
4. Has Mary any eels?
5. Cuthbert arrives Monday: buy onions.
6. Take code books to college.
7. Fly flag for Freda.
8. Send ten chairs to Chester.
9. Contact drives blue car.
10. Martha missed Mary's Morse message.
11. How many fleas on Dan's dog?
12. Put radio on Monday, Olly's on.
13. Leave package at Paddington.

Matchless

1. Cricket is played.
2. Cycling.
3. A style of high-jumping.
4. John McEnroe.
5. Football; they are Sheffield United.
6. Horse racing; he is a jockey.
7. Amateur Swimming Association.
8. Ilie Nastase.
9. Squash.
10. Boats.
11. Hockey.
12. 1976 at Montreal.
13. A score of nought in cricket.
14. American football.
15. Doncaster.
16. Swimming.
17. Show jumping.
18. Rowing.
19. Baseball.
20. Ice skating.
21. Roller skating.
22. Hereford United football team.
23. York City football team.
24. Chris Evert.
25. Winning the Badminton Horse Trials six times (up to 1987).
26. Lacrosse.
27. Swimming.
28. Show jumping.
29. Mountaineering.
30. Fourteen.

They are both football trophies. No. 1 is the Football Association Cup; no. 2 is the World Cup.

1. Golf.
2. Cricket.
3. Rugby.
4. Tennis.
5. Weight-lifting.
6. Fencing.
7. Hockey.
8. Badminton.
9. Lacrosse.
10. Table tennis.

T

The following are false.
3.
7. It is a card game.
8. It is a kind of fruit.
14.
19. It was written by Thomas Hardy.
21. They were held in Athens in 1896.
24. It was George Stephenson.
27. It connects the Atlantic and Pacific Oceans.
29.
31. At least 845 are known to be spoken.
34. It is the Sears Tower in Chicago.
36.
37. It was opened in 1959.
39. It is made from fermented barley or other grains.

Tree Time **175**

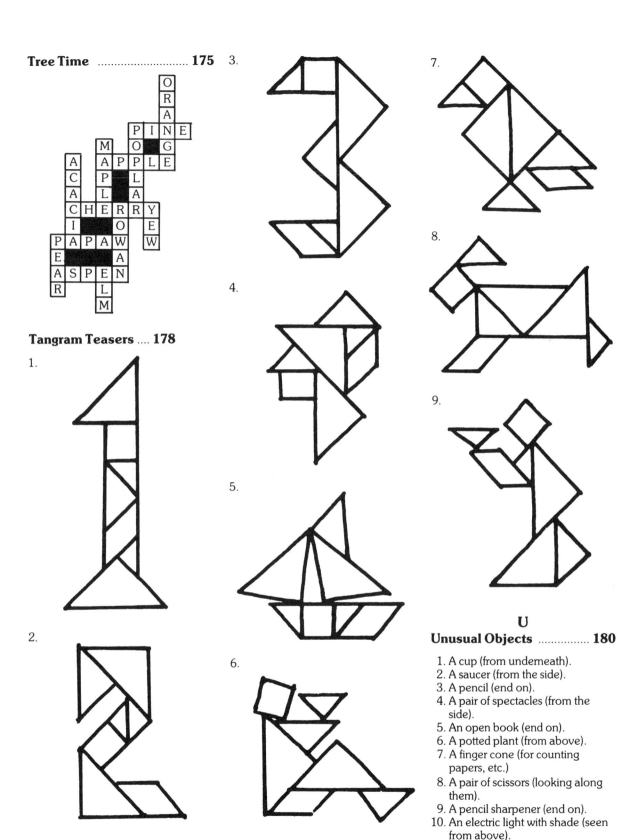

Tangram Teasers **178**

1.

2.

3.

4.

5.

6.

7.

8.

9.

U
Unusual Objects **180**

1. A cup (from underneath).
2. A saucer (from the side).
3. A pencil (end on).
4. A pair of spectacles (from the side).
5. An open book (end on).
6. A potted plant (from above).
7. A finger cone (for counting papers, etc.)
8. A pair of scissors (looking along them).
9. A pencil sharpener (end on).
10. An electric light with shade (seen from above).
11. A wristwatch (end on).

Umbrellas Galore! 184

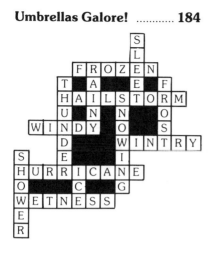

Ulna and Others 185
1. Cervical vertebrae.
2. Clavicle.
3. Sternum.
4. Humerus.
5. Ribs.
6. Ulna.
7. Radius.
8. Lumbar vertebrae.
9. Hip bone.
10. Sacrum.
11. Femur.
12. Patella.
13. Tibia.
14. Fibula.

V

Visual Feast 186
Eye Test
Neither the top step nor the bottom step exists.

Triangle Test
No. It would be impossible to make it out of straight lines as it is drawn — it would have to bend.

Lining Up
Both lines are the same length.

Crazy Object
No — it is impossible to make.

Sign Language
Square no. 7 is the different one, because in all the other squares the plus sign is opposite the minus sign, and the multiplication sign is opposite the division sign.

Parallels Problem
All the lines are parallel with each other except lines 6 and 11.

What's This?
It is all the letters of the alphabet which are made up of straight lines when written as capitals, with one line omitted from each.

Round In Circles — 1
Both circles are the same size.

Angled Question
Both lines are the same length.

Pentangles
35.

A Matter of Distance
Both distances are the same.

Verse and Worse 191
Famous Lines
1. It is one of the many sonnets by William Shakespeare.
2. From 'Hebrew Melodies' by Lord Byron.
3. From 'To a Mouse' by Robert Burns.
4. From 'To a Skylark' by Percy Bysshe Shelley.
5. From 'To Autumn' by John Keats.
6. From 'Leisure' by W. H. Davies.
7. From 'The Princess' by Lord Tennyson.
8. From 'My Garden' by T. E. Brown.

Poets Laureate
John Keats and Philip Larkin.

Hidden Fruits
Fig, hip, date, apple, peach, nectarine, melon, pear, orange, olive, gourd, lemon, raisin.

Vision On 192
Silver Screen Twenty Questions
1. Lions.
2. Alec Guinness.
3. St Trinian's.
4. Clint Eastwood.
5. Cole Porter.
6. Marlon Brando.
7. 1928.
8. Trigger.
9. *Gothic*; Boris Karloff, the most famous Frankenstein of all.
10. Julie Andrews; *The Sound of Music.*
11. *The Gold Rush.*
12. *Singing in the Rain.*
13. Alan Ladd.
14. Ben Kingsley.
15. Michael Caine.
16. Their director, Woody Allen.
17. *Gone With the Wind.*
18. *The Philadelphia Story.*
19. E. M. Forster's.
20. *84 Charing Cross Road.*

Small Screen Twenty Questions
1. Magnus Magnusson.
2. Greendale.
3. *Newsround.*
4. Birmingham.
5. Nick Cotton in *EastEnders.*
6. Robert Robinson.
7. Rod Hull's.
8. Jim Davidson.
9. Lizzie Webb.
10. Kevin the gerbil.
11. Joan Hickson.
12. Krystle in *Dynasty.*
13. The incorrigible civil servant played by Nigel Hawthorne in *Yes, Minister* and *Yes, Prime Minister.*
14. Grace Brothers.
15. John Alderton.
16. Gian Sammarco.
17. Barry Humphries.
18. David Attenborough.
19. Dave Allen.
20. *Blue Peter.*

Famous Faces
1. Wincey Willis.
2. Gyles Brandreth.
3. Una Stubbs.
4. Kenneth Williams.
5. Faith Brown.
6. Lionel Blair.
7. Gloria Hunniford.
8. Christopher Biggins.

Vroom, Vroom 197
There are ten differences.

Voice Over 198

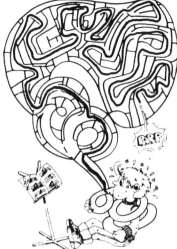

W

Word Play 199
Cat-ch-words
1. Catapult.
2. Scatter.
3. Intricate.
4. Catamaran.
5. Cataract.
6. Catastrophe.
7. Locate.
8. Decathlon.
9. Secateurs.
10. Vacate.

A Man's Rag
1. Punishment.
2. Steamer.
3. Filled.
4. Families.
5. Steaminess.
6. Measured.
7. Waitress.
8. Funeral.
9. Calculate.
10. Destination.

Add an S?
1. Cargoes.
2. Oboes.
3. Operas.
4. Mothers-in-law.
5. Potatoes.
6. Salmon.
7. Oxen.
8. Crises.
9. Mediums (spiritualists) or media (a means of).

10. Teaspoonsful, strictly speaking, but nowadays usually teaspoonfuls.

Male and Female
1. Baroness.
2. Sow.
3. Pen (they are male and female swans).
4. Duck.
5. Countess.
6. Goose.
7. Marchioness.
8. Peahen.
9. Ewe.
10. Queen.

Boys and Girls
1. Arm**ada**.
2. Sul**len**.
3. **Pat**ernal.
4. Sum**mary**.
5. **Bob**bin.
6. Dil**emma**.
7. Pen**ned**.
8. Har**monica**.
9. Sph**eric**al.
10. A**dora**ble.

Spelling Bee
Numbers 5, 7, 9 and 10 are spelt correctly. The other spellings should be as follows:
1. Coolly.
2. Diesel.
3. Fluorescence.
4. Gorilla.
6. Mantelpiece.
8. Rhythm.

What's Wrong? 204
There are six things wrong. The phonograph (a very old-fashioned record player) and the bicycle are both modern inventions and the broom behind the door looks modern, too. The pyramids are in Egypt, but the signpost says they are in Athens, Greece. A Red Indian would feel more at home in North America than in Egypt, and he certainly wouldn't be riding a camel with three humps!

Wool Gathering 205
The shepherd. The wolf cannot reach the sheep.

Worldly Wealth 207
Twelve Square

Ten Triangle
Move the top coin below the bottom row. Then move the two coins at the end of the bottom row to the ends of row 2.

Heads and Tails — 1
The coins are turned over in the following sequence: coins 3 and 4, 4 and 5, 2 and 3.

Heads and Tails — 2
Coins 1 and 2 are moved to the right of coin 6. Coins 6 and 1 are moved to the right of coin 2. Coins 3 and 4 are moved to the right of coin 5.

Coin Cross

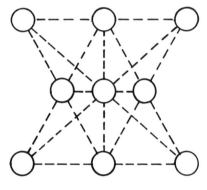

Nine Coins

Three Lines

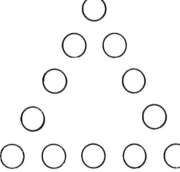

4. A is missing. The proverb is 'Many hands make light work'.
5. O is missing. The proverb is 'Too many cooks spoil the broth'.
6. O is missing. The proverb is 'Never look a gift horse in the mouth'.
7. S is missing. The proverb is 'A rolling stone gathers no moss'.
8. F is missing. The proverb is 'The early bird catches the worm'.
9. T is missing. The proverb is 'A bird in the hand is worth two in the bush'.
10. A, E, I, O and Y are missing. The proverb is 'Early to bed, early to rise, makes a man healthy, wealthy and wise'.

Where in the World?

1. Moscow.
2. New York.
3. River Mississippi.
4. International Dateline.
5. International Dateline.
6. Tropic of Cancer.
7. Equator.
8. Tropic of Capricorn.
9. Peking.
10. Tokyo.
11. Mount Everest.
12. Calcutta.
13. Hong Kong.
14. Dead Sea.
15. Cairo.
16. River Nile.
17. Sydney.
18. Melbourne.
19. Rio de Janeiro.
20. Buenos Aires.
21. Falkland Islands.

X

X Marks the Spot 210

The treasure is hidden under the palm tree at D5. Pudsey Pete will need to use the boat at H5 to cross to the island otherwise the crocodiles will get him.

Wordly Wisdom 209
It's Proverbial

1. A is missing. The proverb is 'A miss is as good as a mile'.
2. L is missing. The proverb is 'Look before you leap'.
3. I is missing. The proverb is 'A stitch in time saves nine'.

Xword Xtra 212

```
S U N D R I E S
W O   N   T
  D E M O N S T R A T E
  A   S   O   N
V I R T U E   S W E D E
  B   N   O   A   L
K I N G A R T H U R   I
  Z   I   I   L   O
A F R I C A     S A T I N
    L   H
```

Xtravaganza! 213

Xperts! 214
1. Campanologist.
2. Trichologist.
3. Horologist.
4. Odontologist.
5. Entomologist.
6. Conchologist.

X Certificates 215
There are seventeen X certificates in the picture.

Xcrutiating! 216
Old and Young
The man was 69 years 12 weeks old; the woman was 30 years 40 weeks old.

Dividing 100
76,   24.

Dotty

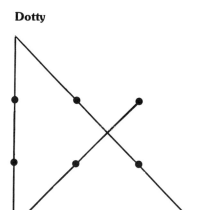

Cider Daze
$46\frac{2}{3}$ days. In one day Mrs Guzzle drinks $\frac{1}{14} - \frac{1}{20} = \frac{3}{140}$ so it takes her $\frac{140}{3}$ days to finish the cider.

Smallest Box
16.

Paintings Puzzle
Kevin K. Kidlington left $\frac{1}{2} + \frac{1}{3} + \frac{1}{9}$ or $\frac{9}{18} + \frac{6}{18} + \frac{2}{18}$ or $\frac{17}{18}$ of his paintings to his children, not *all* his paintings.

Longest River
It doesn't occur at all. The longest river in the world is the Nile.

Pattern Puzzle
The patterns in the top four squares each have the largest symbol in the centre, the smallest on the left, and the medium-sized one on the right. Therefore picture no. 6 in the lower set belongs to the upper four.

Y

Yes or No? 217
1. No. Charlotte Brontë did.
2. Yes. It is also a musical instrument.
3. Yes.
4. Yes.
5. Yes.
6. No, it is used by a carpenter.
7. No, between 1936 and 1939.
8. Yes.
9. Yes.
10. No, forty.
11. Yes.
12. No, it means 'pen name'.
13. Yes.
14. No, a make of car.
15. Yes.
16. No, it was a lighthouse, and one of the Seven Wonders of the ancient world.
17. Yes.
18. Yes.
19. No, it is the passage from the mouth to the stomach.
20. Yes.

Yellow, Green, Blue 218
The colours of the rainbow are red, orange, yellow, green, blue, indigo, violet.

Y's Words 219

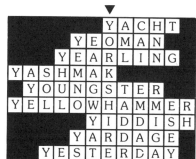

Planet Ywho 220
Squares A4, D10 and F2 are identical.

There are thirteen bug-eyed monsters and twelve robots in the picture.

Y, OY? 222
1. I see you are in today.
2. Please may I go to the fair?
3. Does the bus stop here?
4. How are you?
5. Jean's aunt has an apple tree.

Z

Zoo Time 223
Zoo Quiz
1. Dogs.
2. A draught horse.
3. Jersey and Guernsey cows.
4. A parrot.
5. Hyena — the other two are members of the cat family.
6. The cuckoo.
7. True.
8. The eel.
9. Yes.
10. Apes.
11. The fox.
12. The salamander.
13. No, one.
14. Types of butterfly.
15. 40 mph (64 km/h).
16. False.
17. The goldcrest.
18. A chicken.
19. A creature that can live either on land or in water.
20. Types of deer.

Zoo Words
1. Sly, spiteful.
2. Stupid or flighty.
3. With keen eyesight.
4. Large, clumsy or unwieldy.
5. Quick-tempered.
6. Scolding.
7. Morose, irritable.
8. Timid, colourless or shy person.
9. Stupid and slow.
10. Stubborn.
11. Conceited.
12. Crazy.
13. Bashful.
14. Obstinate, persistent.
15. Slow-moving, lazy.
16. Irritable, ill-tempered.

Animal Homes
River
Beaver, kingfisher, otter, trout, vole.
Pond
Carp, frog, newt, toad, water snail.
Woodland
Badger, deer, rook, squirrel, woodpecker.
Mountains
Eagle, goat, wolf.
Grassland
Hare, horse, rabbit, skylark.

1 — E; 2 — D; 3 — A; 4 — H; 5 — I;
6 — G; 7 — F; 8 — B; 9 — C.

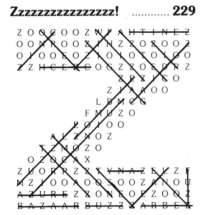

Index

Subject Index